OUR
AMERICAN
EXPERIMENT

Author of THE RADICAL DECLARATION
BYRON WILLIAMS

TABLE of CONTENTS

ALSO by BYRON WILLIAMS

Strip Mall Patriotism: Moral Reflection of the Iraq War

1963: The Year of Hope and Hostility (First Edition)

Solitaire: Magda Goebbels:
A Banality of Ambition and Evil

Radical Declaration: An Enlightened American Idea

This book is dedicated to the memory of my father,
Henry Rayford Cheatham.

It was his profound love and belief in me
that made this work possible.

*"The evil that men do, lives after them,
the good is oft' interred with their bones."*

~ Frederick Douglass 1852 ~

INTRODUCTION

Writing a collection of short stories is more than a series of allegories designed to appease the time-strapped. Quite the contrary; they can serve as the opening salvo to prod the reader to think deeply about the issue presented. But rather than a potpourri of short yarns, they require a through line that binds the stories. Though disparate on the surface, they bear a commonality.

What is the through line for *Our American Experiment*? Influenced by the absurdity championed by French philosopher, Albert Camus, along with the paradox found in the writings of theologian, Reinhold Niebuhr, *Our American Experiment* examines many of the issues that confront 21st-century America through the lens of fiction. It is an attempt to go beyond the binary cacophony that too often dominates public discourse.

Issues such as abortion, the death penalty, unbridled political ambition, racism, LGBT equality, and others that dominate our public discourse often ignore the requisite nuance. The result has left us marred in absurdity and paradox.

As Camus offers, absurdity is the conflict between the human tendency to seek inherent value in the meaning of life, coupled with our collective inability to realize it with any degree of satisfaction that results in the promotion of certainty. In this context, certainty becomes the false refuge for those that claim their version of America is "THE" version. Anyone that does not subscribe to this vision is excluded from the vaunted mainstream.

Paradox is the silent third party within the American narrative that represents the distance between the perfection of our stated precepts and the imperfection associated with its execution. When we portray our certainty as unimpeachable, we do so with the comfort of ignoring the paradox that roams unabated.

Each of the stories selected offers an opening vignette for a frame of reference. But I leave the discovery of the absurdity and the paradox to the reader's exploration. Part 2 consists of four nonfiction essays that examine America's perennial intractable challenge.

Whether fiction or nonfiction, we are challenged by the words of William Dean Howells, who offered, *"What the American public wants in the theater is a tragedy with a happy ending."* Assuming the validity of what would otherwise be deemed as an oxymoron, we can ill afford to examine issues critical to the American experience void of their complexity. To do so will lead to our collective peril.

~ **BW**

Notes: The fiction section is an examination of contemporary American issues. Each story is a work of the author's imagination. Any resemblance of any character to a real, living person is merely a coincidence.

PART
I

CHAPTER 1

The Plus Sign

Prior to the Supreme Court overturning of Roe v. Wade, the Texas abortion law enacted in 2021 was the inspiration for this story.

On September 1, 2021, Senate Bill 8 (SB 8) went into effect in the state of Texas. Sometimes referred to as the "heartbeat bill," SB 8 banned abortions after six weeks—a time period that concludes before most women know they're pregnant. Moreover, SB 8 provided no exceptions for rape or incest. The most controversial aspect of the legislation was the provision that authorized members of the public to sue anyone who performs or facilitates an illegal abortion for a minimum of $10,000 in statutory damages per abortion, plus court costs and attorneys' fees. Since SB 8 was passed, Dobbs v. Jackson overturned the landmark Supreme Court ruling in Roe v. Wade.

Though SB 8 was the inspiration, this is a story about the subjectivity of personal morality.

SHARON STOOD ALONE in her bathroom, staring at the plus sign on her home pregnancy test. The only thing missing were the trumpets blaring and a recorded voice emanating through a bullhorn to announce to her neighbors: "Sharon Ross, the 19-year-old daughter of Texas' ultra conservative state senator, Randolph Ross, is indeed pregnant in the first semester of her freshman year at Southern Methodist University!"

Sharon's father had authored the nation's most onerous abortion law. Senate Bill 8 banned all abortions after six weeks. There were no exceptions for rape, incest, or the mother's health. According to Senator Ross, "The rights of the unborn will be protected in the Lone Star State!"

The law was already in effect. The U.S. Supreme Court denied the petition for an injunction without bothering to hear arguments or read briefings. After the Court's decision, Senator Ross issued a statement: "It's a great day for the state of Texas!"

Still staring at the plus sign, Sharon thought about her father's words. She didn't believe they were intended to include his only daughter but how would Senator Ross feel if he knew the father of Sharon's child was not a white evangelical Christian, but a member of the SMU basketball team? What would this do to his moral crusade that he vowed would, "sweep across Texas like the winds of the prairie?" Sharon remembered how her father would always end his political stump speeches by declaring: "The coastal elites have no place in Texas."

Before she found herself paralyzed in the bathroom with the plus sign staring her in the face, Sharon had not given much thought to her father's stand on reproductive rights. Hoping to uncover a loophole in the fine print, she reached into the wastebasket for the pregnancy test instructions. But instead of hope, she realized further confirmation.

Already thinking about the nexus between her newfound physical reality and her father's politics, she said, "This damn test is 99% accurate, that doesn't leave much room for error. And the last time I had a period was more than six weeks ago."

Her first impulse was to terminate the pregnancy. Being a mother at 20 was not part of her future plans. That decision could also sever her relationship with her father, who she adored. But then the Texas law reminded her that the choice to terminate her pregnancy was not available. Suddenly, the adored father became the tangible symbol representing a group of lawmakers in the State Capitol that prematurely stood proxy for her choice. The shock notwithstanding, she realized there was someone she needed to inform.

"I've got to tell Jonathan!"

Jonathan Bryant—a sophomore and the leading scorer on the SMU basketball team. He was popular around campus, a good student, and well-liked. His buzzer-beater against rival Rice University cemented his legacy within the SMU community. Jonathan grew up in the South Oak Cliff section of Dallas. His father was a postal worker and his mother was a beautician. He also had two older brothers that helped to hone his skills on the basketball court.

Picking up her iPhone, "Siri, call Jonathan," Sharon said.

After two rings, Jonathan predictably answered, "Hey there, I was just about to call you to see if you wanted to get together later?"

"I do. Actually, could you come over now?"

"That sounds serious."

"I need to share something with you and I don't want to do it over the phone."

"You're pregnant, aren't you?" Jonathan remarked.

"Just come over, we can talk then," she said.

"I'm on my way."

It was only a 10-minute drive for Jonathan to get to Sharon's uptown apartment. Because they spent more time at her apartment than at his studio near the campus, Sharon had already provided him with the code for entrance through the secured gate. Not bothering to wait for the elevator, he raced up the stairs to the third floor. With anxiety dictating his movements, his knock on the door felt more like the pounding of someone who was one step away from forced entry.

Sharon could already sense Jonathan was uneasy. She answered the door, and in an attempt to lighten the mood, she blurted, "Well, that was quick! Is this what I have to do to get you to be on time when we go out?"

"I know you, I can feel when something is wrong," he said.

Still trying to lower Jonathan's anxiety, Sharon sarcastically asked, "Is that why you didn't bother to shower before coming over? You're still sweaty from your workout... or did my phone call do that?"

"Haha! Very funny!" Jonathan sarcastically said. "But I know something is wrong!"

Jonathan's obvious concern was comforting for Sharon. She found it subliminally reassuring that she would not be alone.

"C'mon, Sharon, I know something is wrong," he said.

"Well, why don't you sit down?"

Sitting on her sofa, Sharon organically broke the invisible line of closeness that suggests intimacy. Gently taking Jonathan's hand, looking him tenderly in the eye, she said, "You were right… I am pregnant."

Letting out a huge sigh, Jonathan said, "That's a relief!"

"A relief?" Sharon said.

Recognizing the awkwardness of his remark, Jonathan said, "I thought you were pregnant, but driving over here, I thought of other possibilities."

"Like what?"

"I thought maybe you might be breaking up with me. Then I thought you might have cancer or COVID. So, being pregnant was not the worst thing."

Sharon, looking at Jonathan with a faint smile, thought to herself, *That was the dumbest, clumsiest, and probably the sweetest thing anyone has ever said to me.*

The smile Sharon attempted to muster could no longer hold back the raging emotions of fear and confusion that flooded her soul.

Tearful, she fell onto his lap, "Oh, Jonathan, I'm so scared. I don't know what to do."

Rubbing the side of her face, Jonathan said softly, "Whatever you decide, I will be with you."

"Thank you. I cannot tell you how much that means

to me, but do you know what you're getting into?"

"I do."

"Do you really? Did you forget who my father is? Did you somehow forget that he is the author of the worst abortion law in the country? Plus, I'm passed the six-week point so I don't see how there will be an abortion."

"Then we'll get married."

Sharon raised her head in disbelief. She was touched that Jonathan said all the right things, but in her soul, she felt they would prove to be wrong.

"You want to marry me?"

"Absolutely!"

"No one in my family knows you exist. Based on what you've told me, I'm a secret in the Bryant home, so how's that going to work when we show up married?"

"Work for who... your family? My family? It doesn't have to work for them, it just has to work for us!"

"You make it sound so easy."

"It is that easy."

In the midst of her uncertainty and confusion, she had never felt closer to Jonathan. His tenderness and support made her feel whatever happened, there would be light at the end of the tunnel. She also thought about her father. She knew that he would be more outraged by Jonathan's presence than the fact she was pregnant at 19.

Trembling, she asked, "Is it really as easy as you say?"

"Yes, as long as we have each other," Jonathan responded.

"Then I accept. Yes, Jonathan Raphael Bryant, I will

marry you."

"You can't do it like that," he said.

Jonathan popped up from the sofa. "Stand up," he said.

As she stood up, Jonathan took her hand, dropping to a single knee. With both fighting back tears, Jonathan, looking squarely in her eyes, said, "Sharon Maria Ross, make me the happiest man on earth by becoming my wife."

Dropping to her knees, Sharon blurted, "Yes!" Their embrace morphed into a long, passionate kiss.

Sharon, pulling back slightly, chuckled, "I know what's on your mind right now because it's on mine, but we have to deal with the hard part."

"I know, we have to tell our families," he said.

"Yes."

"When do you think we should do it?"

"Why don't I tell my parents next weekend and you tell yours the week after?"

"Do you want me to come with you?"

"I do, but I think it best that I go alone."

"If you say so."

"Jonathan, I do have another request…"

"What is it?"

"Will you stay with me until I go back home to Odessa next week? I know you have to work out, but I was hoping that you could do…"

Jonathan gently placed his hand over Sharon's mouth.

"There's nothing else to say, I will stay with you."

Jonathan's comforting words led to another

passionate kiss. This time, there were no interruptions — no pauses for reflective thoughts. Never before had Sharon felt so safe, so loved, and never before had she felt someone had seen her for who she truly was. Mentally as well as physically, she was completely open to Jonathan.

As the week progressed, Sharon wished it would never reach its conclusion. Her appointment with a Dallas gynecologist confirmed the findings of the home pregnancy test. But rather than the consternation she felt staring at the plus sign in her bathroom, she felt composure, an inner joy made possible by Jonathan's reaction to the news. On Wednesday afternoon, Jonathan returned to her apartment after practice. Sharon was looking out the window contemplating her life. He walked behind her, gently placing a piano wood ring box in her left hand. Opening it slowly, Sharon gazed at the single-carat diamond ring. Once again, Jonathan, dropping to one knee, took her by her right hand, simply saying, "This will make it official."

Sharon was overcome by tears of joy, never had she felt love in such an authentic way. Sliding the ring on the third finger of her left hand, it fit perfectly. Sharon exclaimed, "How did you know my ring size?"

With a sly confident smile, Jonathan replied, "Don't worry about it."

The trepidation she felt about becoming a mother lessened. But it was also a false reality. The trip back home to Odessa was drawing near. If she could stay in Jonathan's arms and ignore the outside world, everything would work itself out.

"Are you sure you don't want me to go with you to Odessa?" Jonathan asked.

"I'm sure. I really want you there, but if you come, it will only make things worse."

"Because of your father?" Jonathan asked.

"Yes, because of my father."

With the seriousness of the issue growing, Jonathan asked somewhat hesitantly, "What will your mother say?"

"It doesn't matter," Sharon said dryly.

"What do you mean it doesn't matter?"

"What matters to my mother is that the liquor cabinet is well stocked with gin."

Quickly changing the subject, Sharon asked, "What will your family say?"

Feigning naiveté, Jonathan replied, "Say about what?"

"The prospects of Troy Aikman returning to play quarterback for the Dallas Cowboys next season! I think you know what I'm talking about!" Sharon snapped.

"They probably won't like it at first, but I'm sure the good people at my mom's church will help her see the light and she will bring my father along. My brothers won't care, and no one else matters."

Sharon then asked, "Will it matter that I'm a—"

Abruptly cutting her off, "It won't matter," Jonathan replied confidently.

"I wish I could say that, but I know it will matter. At least it will matter to my father."

The drive from Dallas to Odessa was not exactly scenic beauty. Going through metropolitan areas such as

Abilene, Big Spring, and Midland made the five-hour drive feel much longer. But it was a great drive if one needed time to think. Sharon played out the conversation with her parents in her head, anticipating her father's reaction and her mother's inaction. There were parts of the conversation that would be predictable. Her father would be angry about her being pregnant and not married, angrier that it was Jonathan, but angrier still about how this would make him look.

Sharon pulled into the long, sweeping driveway of her family's six-bedroom, 17,000-square-foot home that sat on an additional 70 acres. She tried to imagine Jonathan accompanying her at any point, but she couldn't. She knew at that moment whatever decision she made would probably result in a choice between her parents and Jonathan.

Her father, having already seen her pulling up, walked to the car with a sense of excitement. Slipping off her engagement ring, Sharon dropped it in the car ashtray, then immediately jumped out of the car to greet her father. Though it had been roughly 90 days since she left for SMU, she remained his little girl. As he embraced his daughter, he cried out, "Peanut," his name for her since she was a baby. "We didn't expect you until Thanksgiving, but I'm so glad you're here. The house has been so quiet without you!"

"Hello, Daddy!" Sharon responded cheerfully.

Then he paused, "Why are you here? You didn't get kicked out of school already?"

Chuckling, Sharon said, "No, Daddy! I just wanted to spend some time with you."

"Every time you want to spend some time with me, it is usually a very expensive time," he said. Quickly adding, "I know, you maxed out your credit cards. How much do you need?"

Amused at her father's curiosity, Sharon said, "Daddy, you told me when I left for school that you were just a phone call away if I needed anything. Plus, that's why God created Cash App so I wouldn't have to take that dreary dusty drive from Dallas to Odessa. I do have some news, but it can wait. Where's Momma?"

"She's in the kitchen," her father said.

The "kitchen" was the long-established euphemism denoting that Sharon's mother was drinking.

Undeterred, Sharon entered the front, "Momma, where are you?" With the aid of the high ceilings, Sharon's voice reverberated throughout the house.

A voice from upstairs could be heard saying, "Baby, is that you?"

"Yes, Momma, it's me!"

Walking down the steps of their luxurious spiral staircase was a frail woman adorning an emerald green silk robe that partially concealed her pink, one-piece pullover silk nightgown. Years of drinking gave Eugenia Ross a glazed look, reminiscent of Norma Desmond from the movie *Sunset Boulevard*. It hurt Sharon to see her mother that way, who appeared even more frail than the last time she saw her. She cringed as she felt Eugenia's rib cage when they hugged.

"Oh, baby, it's so good to see you," her mother said. Echoing her husband's sentiments, she added, "The house is so empty without you."

Sharon was the only authentic thing her parents had in common. With her gone, they only had Senator Ross' attempts to portray their marriage as consistent with the family values image he purported as one of Texas' leading conservative voices.

"Now, why are you here? With all the things happening on that SMU campus and in Dallas, I know you didn't drive five hours just to see old people pretending to be self-righteous."

This was a side of her mother that Sharon was unfamiliar with. She always assumed her mother was oblivious to what was going on daily, but her perceptive insight surprised and pleased Sharon.

"Well, Momma, I need to talk with y'all."

Pulling away from Sharon, she said softly, "Just a minute, baby."

Walking to the large mahogany double entry doors, Eugenia opened it halfway and yelled out, "Randy, get in here, Sharon needs to talk with us."

"Oh, not now, Momma!"

"You need to talk, right?"

"Yes!"

"If you wait for a couple of hours, will you need to talk?"

"Yes!"

"Well, hell, we might as well talk now!"

"Yes, Ma'am."

"Where is your daddy?" Pausing momentarily, Eugenia said, "Just a minute, sweetheart!"

She went back to the door, and this time, stood completely outside, "Goddammit, Randy, didn't you hear me say Sharon wants to talk with us? There ain't no fucking conservative Christians to be found in those weeds."

Looking at Sharon as she came back into the house, Eugenia said, "I swear your daddy can be slower than a slug in January when there ain't no cameras or voters around."

Storming into the house, Randolph shouted at Eugenia, "Why do you have to speak like that outside?"

"Why? You worried that some of your Bible belt hussies might be hidden somewhere in the weeds on my daddy's 70 acres, costing you some votes?" Eugenia shot back.

Randolph hated when Eugenia reminded him of the source of his wealth, but there was little he could say. He was more interested in developing a conservative persona that could one day have him in the governor's seat in Austin; and that couldn't happen without Eugenia at his side in spite of her drinking, which was one of the worst-kept secrets in Odessa.

"Randy, I understand that your holier than thou knickers are in a twist, but this ain't about you. Our daughter needs to talk with us," Eugenia said.

Turning to Sharon, Eugenia said, "Let's go into the study."

The study, with its dark wood paneling, hardwood floors, and long leather couch and accompanying chairs was the most intimate place in the home. Perfect for what Sharon had to say.

Randolph and Eugenia sat together on the couch, and Sharon sat in one of the leather chairs that were facing them.

"Well, there is no easy way to say this, so I might as well just come out and say it. I'm pregnant," Sharon said.

Without pausing to take the temperature in the room, Randolph blurted out, "How many weeks?"

Understanding that his question was related to the abortion legislation that he authored, Sharon calmly said, "More than six weeks, Daddy!"

With a look of utter contempt, Eugenia said, "Our daughter needs us and the first thing on your fucking mind is that goddamn stupid piece of legislation and how this may impact how you look publicly?"

Exhibiting a modicum of contrition, Randolph said, "That's not what I meant... not what I meant to say. I meant to ask, 'Does the father know about this?'"

"Yes, Daddy, he knows."

"And what are his feelings?"

"He wants to marry me."

"That's great, when do we get to meet him?"

"You don't know anything about him," Sharon said.

"I know that you're pregnant. I know you told the father, who has taken steps to do the right thing, the moral thing. Frankly, it is the only thing one can do in this situation. I wish our society had more like him," Randolph said.

"Baby, do you love the boy?" Eugenia asked.

"Yes, Ma'am!" Eugenia responded.

"Do you believe the boy loves you?"

"Oh, yes. He makes me feel special."

"Then what is it, baby? What's the problem?" Eugenia asked.

"Where did you meet him?" Randolph asked.

"He's a sophomore at SMU," Sharon replied.

"What does he study?" Randolph asked.

"He's leaning toward history, he wants to become a lawyer."

"That's good!" Randolph said. "I for one definitely want to meet him, I have contacts throughout the state, but especially in Dallas that could pave the way for an enterprising young man like you've described. What's his name?"

Reluctantly, Sharon said, "Jonathan."

"Jonathan what?"

"Jonathan Bryant."

An ashen look quickly came across Randolph's face. He was not only an alum of SMU, but also an active athletic booster. Randolph was well-acquainted with the name Jonathan Bryant but was hoping it was not the one he had in mind. Tepidly, Randolph asked, "Not the basketball player?"

With a short sigh, Sharon said, "Yes, Daddy, the basketball player."

"Oh, this is a problem," Randolph sighed.

Bewildered, Eugenia asked, "Why is it all of a sudden there is a problem with who this young man is?"

"Eugenia!" Randolph shouted. "Do you remember the boy that hit the game winning-shot against Rice last year?"

"Yes."

"THAT'S JONATHAN BRYANT!" Randolph exclaimed.

"Oh my! Just imagine what Malvina Johnson would

do with that information. Her daddy always hated my daddy," Eugenia mumbled as she reached for the bottle of gin that was conveniently nearby.

Though not surprised, having seen this movie throughout her life, Sharon sat disappointed as the conversation went from her announcing that she was pregnant to Jonathan's wonderful qualifications to it now being her parents' problem. At no time did anyone inquire about her mental or physical state.

Randolph's animated gestures and decibel level seized control of the conversation as Eugenia retreated to the refuge of alcohol. Sharon was a passive onlooker who was demoted from the subject of the sentence to a modifier that unleashed her parents' dysfunctional behavior.

"Peanut," Randolph said softly. "This thing threw me for a spin, I don't mean to sound insensitive. I truly don't. Would you mind if I spoke to your mother in private for about 15 minutes?"

"No, Daddy, I don't mind."

Leaving the study, Sharon returned to her room. Thinking to herself, *Daddy is never going to accept Jonathan and I cannot turn my back on my family. Can I have this baby alone? And will anybody in Odessa want to be with me and a biracial child?*

Sharon's love for Jonathan felt different outside the bubble of the SMU surroundings. She loved Jonathan and wanted him, but she also feared stepping outside the gravitational pull of her parents'—primarily Randolph's—approval. And she certainly didn't want to be the reason that caused Randolph not to achieve his political aspirations.

But what could she do? Marry Jonathan and lose her family? Have the baby and become a pariah in Odessa? Anywhere Sharon went with the baby, with or without Jonathan, she would be alone. She would not have her parents' emotional or financial support. It was a world she didn't know, and quite frankly, possessed no interest in becoming acquainted.

Sharon also knew that if she stayed with Jonathan, Randolph would make his life miserable, at least in the state of Texas. He would take their being together as a personal affront to everything Randolph stood for. Probably the first thing Randolph would do is work to get Jonathan's scholarship revoked. Though Jonathan was SMU's best player, his basketball prowess would prove no match for the power of Texas politics. Without adequate notification, she was no longer "Peanut," just one burdened with adult decisions that her 19 years in Odessa had not equipped her. Whatever the decision, pain for someone would be the predictable outcome.

Nothing was settled, but Sharon had resigned herself that she would not return to Dallas, at least not for the foreseeable future. And she needed to inform Jonathan of her decision.

"Siri, call Jonathan," she said.

Jonathan predictably answered after two rings.

"Hey there," he said enthusiastically. "I was just thinking about you, how's it going?"

"Okay, I guess," Sharon responded

"What's wrong?" Jonathan asked.

"Why would you say something is wrong?"

"The tone in your voice did!"

Jonathan's last statement underscored Sharon's attraction to him. His intuitive perception of her was at times unnerving, but it never ceased to remind Sharon that Jonathan saw her authentically, in a manner no one else had.

"Once again, you're right. There's no easy way to say this, but I'm not coming back to Dallas any time soon."

Like a sharp elbow to the solar plexus, Jonathan lost his breath.

"WHAT?" he exclaimed.

"I've thought about it and it seems like the best answer," Sharon said.

"Best for who? It's certainly not the best answer for me!" Jonathan responded.

"Actually, it is the best answer for you," Sharon said.

"How so?"

"Jonathan, I've thought about it and it simply won't work between us... our worlds are just too different," Sharon admitted.

"In other words, your father is never going to accept us being together," Jonathan lamented.

"Yes, my father is never going to accept it."

"And the baby?"

"I don't know!" Sharon responded curtly.

"What do you mean you don't know?"

"Jonathan, I just know that I'm not coming back to school. I have not thought beyond that."

"What about us?"

"There is no "us"! There can't be."

"You don't believe that. I can hear it in your voice."

"It doesn't matter what I believe or what you think you hear. I'm sorry!"

Sharon abruptly ended the conversation. She had told herself breaking up with Jonathan was the right thing to do, but it didn't feel that way. Less so with every repeated attempt by Jonathan to call her back. Turning her phone off didn't help. She didn't need to take Jonathan's call to know what he would say. His voice kept ringing in her head.

"Sharon, you don't have to do this. I know you want to be with me as much as I want to be with you. It doesn't matter what your father thinks, we can work it out. I love you."

Thinking about Jonathan's words, Sharon mumbled, "I love you too!" Lying on her bed, there was a knock on Sharon's door.

"Baby, are you in there? It's your mother. Your father wants to talk with you in the study."

"Okay, Momma."

Sharon opened the door; Eugenia was still standing there. A look of consternation enveloped her gaunt face. Taking Sharon by the hand, Eugenia said softly, "Baby, whatever happens, we're going to get through this. Me and your daddy love you, don't ever forget that."

Since her conversation with Jonathan, Sharon had become increasingly numb to the events around her. Looking at Eugenia during her compassionate affirmation, Sharon said nothing. Walking down the steps, she kept replaying her conversation with Jonathan in her mind. When Sharon entered the study, she was surprised to be greeted by her "daddy," instead of State Senator Randolph Ross.

"How are you doing, Peanut?"

"I've had better days," Sharon responded.

"Well, I've got some news for you… if you keep on livin', you might have some days worse than this."

"I don't see how."

"You can't see how, not until they arrive. But trust me, that's how life works."

"Daddy, Momma said you wanted to talk with me."

Randolph was somewhat caught off guard by Sharon's directness, putting a premature end to his attempts at a charm offensive.

"Your mother and I talked and decided that you should see my friend, Dr. Joel Myers, for a thorough examination. He's a gynecologist in San Clemente, California. You and I can leave tomorrow. I've already spoken with Joel and he'll see you the following day."

"Daddy, are you saying what I think you're saying?"

"I'm saying you and I will fly to California tomorrow to see Dr. Myers for a thorough examination. Nothing else needs to be said."

"Daddy, I need some time."

"You don't have any time. I've already printed out the boarding passes. The car service will be here at 6:00 AM to pick us up," Randolph said.

"Daddy, doesn't this go against what you believe, what you've built your career on?"

"What I believe for my constituents doesn't necessarily mean it applies to this house. Besides, you'd be surprised to know how many of my constituents would agree with my decision if they found out Jonathan Bryant was the father."

Sharon had been mistaken—she was having a meeting with Sen. Ross, who was merely using "Daddy" as an initial façade.

"When we return, we should probably get you enrolled at Abilene Christian University," Randolph added.

Randolph's last comment was the punishment for Jonathan. SMU was hardly the bastion of left-leaning propaganda, but through Sharon's eyes, Abilene Christian was the outer bank of conservatism. Moreover, it was smaller and easier for Randolph to keep tabs on Sharon.

"Okay, Daddy," she said.

As Sharon left the study, she turned back toward Randolph, "Ever since I was a child I've read about the intimidating atmosphere that accompanied a meeting with Senator Randolph Ross. I never thought I would experience it at a time when I so needed to talk with my daddy."

Returning to her room, Sharon wasn't certain that she wanted to have a baby, but she detested that Randolph had made a unilateral decision. She also felt resentment about succumbing to the pressure to break up with Jonathan. She knew she did not possess the strength to stand up to her father and was ashamed of her weakness. It was at that moment, for the first time she questioned the fallacy of her first 19 years of life.

Sharon thought just how much her life had changed

since she pulled into her parents' driveway. The excitement that greeted her had been replaced by a hypocritical decision, belying the conservative politics that her father championed. The plan that her parents demanded would ensure that she continued to be a Ross in good standing. And within two days, every member of the Ross family could return to their dysfunctional silos and society would be none the wiser. This was how it had always been in the Ross household. Sharon had to become pregnant, out of wedlock, by someone deemed undesirable to understand her role in the family.

Randolph wouldn't give it a second thought; Eugenia would most likely store it in her intoxicated cloud, unlikely to feel the need to download it. But Sharon knew she would not be able to forget. Already aware of the pain she caused Jonathan, who was guilty of nothing except a desire to love her. She had no way to predict if a relationship with Jonathan would have worked long-term—there would certainly be more factors working against them. But each step she took returning to her room, against her better judgment, cemented Sharon's commitment to remain a Ross in good standing with all rights and privileges pertaining despite its associated dysfunction.

Sharon quietly walked back to her room. Eugenia's bedroom door, which was across from Sharon's room, was cracked open and the light was on. Sharon took a step toward her mother's door to check on her, but decided against it.

"Is that you, baby?"

"Yes, Momma."

"Come on in here, I want to speak to you for a moment."

Her mother's uncharacteristic request compelled Sharon to enter what she assumed would be an intoxicated soliloquy. It was, but not what Sharon expected.

"I know my drinking bothers you, and it should... sometimes it bothers me," her mother said. "But let me share with you why I drink, and at this point in my life, why I will continue to drink until the Lord calls me home."

"Momma, we don't have to go into this now," Sharon said.

"We do have to go into it now because your life depends on it. I don't want you to end up like me."

Sharon was surprised by her mother's response. Rarely did she speak with such assurance, and never after consuming gin. Sharon warily walked to the foot of the bed and sat down.

"You don't know why I drink; your father doesn't know why I drink. It's been a secret that I kept buried in my heart. It's too late for me, but not for my only child, who, in my moments of clarity, I love beyond measure. In the book of Ezekiel, it says, 'I sat, where they sat.' My darling, I've sat where you're sitting right now."

Sharon sat motionless.

"You don't remember Papa Joe, your grandfather, my daddy?" Eugenia asked.

"No, Ma'am."

"You were just a baby when he died. But before I gave birth to you, I had gotten pregnant when I was about your age by one of the ranch hands. Not only was he a ranch hand… he was a Jew. But I loved him. When my daddy found out, he sent me to New York to get it taken care of. When I returned, that boy was gone. I never heard from him again. From that time on, his name was never uttered on the ranch."

"Is that why you drink?" Sharon asked.

"I thought it was, but now I'm not so sure."

"What do you mean?"

"When you said you were pregnant and I found out who that Jonathan was, I felt just like my daddy."

"So, you're okay with Daddy taking me to California in the morning?"

"It was my idea," Eugenia said coldly.

"Yours?" Sharon said, surprised.

"Yes, mine. My daddy was right to send me away, and your daddy is right to take you to California in the morning."

Full of emotion, Sharon screamed, "HOW CAN YOU SAY SOMETHING LIKE THAT? MY WORLD IS TURNED UPSIDE DOWN AND YOU'RE TRYING TO GIVE ME SOME PREVENTATIVE CARE NOT TO END UP A DRUNK LIKE YOU?"

"That's exactly what I'm doing," Eugenia said calmly.

"I've wasted so many years feeling sorry for myself, not knowing there were those more mature than me that knew my best interests. I'm sure this Jonathan is a nice boy, but it could never work. And you toting a baby around that doesn't look like you wouldn't work either, especially here in Odessa."

"Why do you think I would stay in Odessa?"

"Because this is your legacy, just as it was mine. I was too stupid to see it, but it's not too late for you," Eugenia said.

"What if I don't want it?" Sharon shot back.

"It doesn't matter, it's bigger than you. I tried to drink it away and it's still here," Eugenia said.

Sharon had no interest in being a catharsis for Eugenia's decades of self-destruction. As far as she was concerned, her legacy was delineated between before she arrived back in Odessa and after, and Eugenia's was before the bottle and after.

As her mother continued with increasingly incomprehensible babble, replenishing her glass with gin, Sharon saw the answer to her dilemma resting at the foot of her mother's bed. It was her mother's favorite leather handbag—it was open. Inside the handbag, Sharon could see the small bottle that contained her mother's prescription painkillers. Those pills represented the end to all of Sharon's worries.

Those pills would put an end to any unrealistic expectations held for Sharon to become a Ross in good standing. She wouldn't have to concern herself with catching the plane to California in the morning or be quarantined for the next several years at Abilene Christian. Those pills would bridge the gap between the image of an idyllic family and the reality of the paradox and hypocrisy that dwelled just below the surface. Never again would she hurt Jonathan with her words, although the pain he would undoubtedly experience in the immediate aftermath would be part of the unintended consequences of her actions. Those pills would end Sharon's dilemma between what she wanted and what Eugenia thought was her rightful place, and most importantly, those pills would protect her father's reputation as Texas' champion of the unborn. Rather than the binary options presented by her mother, those pills represented a third way. If being a Ross meant having to sacrifice something for the greater good, then Sharon saw her purpose tucked away in Eugenia's leather handbag.

As Sharon got up to return to her room, her mother called out, "Sharon, did you hear what I said?"

"Yes, Mama, I heard you. Thank you for finally sharing with me that the qualifications for being a Ross meant that everyone had a price they must be willing to pay. The price is higher for some than others, but we all must pay," Sharon said.

Oblivious to Sharon's last comment, an increasingly inebriated Eugenia said, "It may not always feel like it, but your daddy loves you!"

"Yes, Momma, I know. And I love him."

With that, Sharon left her mother's bedroom. The leather handbag still sat at the foot of her mother's bed, but now it was closed.

CHAPTER 2

Not Guilty

Pudd'nhead Wilson is an 1894 novel written by Mark Twain. It is a yarn that centers around two boys—one born into slavery, with 1/32 black ancestry; the other white, born to be the master of the house. The two boys look similar but are switched in infancy. Each grows into the other's social role.

This is the inspiration for Not Guilty. It raises the question: What if Kyle Rittenhouse was black? Rittenhouse, then 17, killed two individuals and injured another during the 2020 civil unrest in Kenosha, Wisconsin. He was found not guilty of any criminal charges.

ON THE MORNING of January 6, 2021, Jamal Robinson was angry and he was prepared to do something about it. From his home in Bethesda, Maryland, the 17-year-old Robinson was aware of a planned demonstration in the nation's Capitol, protesting what some concluded was a stolen election. One week earlier, Jamal, a high school senior, had enlisted in the Marine Corps and was to begin basic training once he graduated from high school in June. He saw serving in the Marines as a way to give back a portion of what the country had given to him.

But his country needed him immediately—at least that's how Jamal saw it. America was potentially under assault by what he deemed a band of misguided insurrectionists, who were the patriotic equivalent of Benedict Arnold and Timothy McVeigh that sought to undermine America's long-standing tradition of a peaceful transfer of power.

Jamal quickly made a call.

The voice on the other end said, "Hey, what's up, little brother!"

"I need to stop by for a minute."

"Why?"

"Will you be there in 30 minutes?"

"No, I won't be here!"

The voice on the other end immediately signed off, but Jamal knew it was a code to stop by and pick up the semi-automatic handgun that was technically his, but he was too young to own one in Maryland or DC. Moreover, the 30-minute time frame was to give the voice on the phone time to leave the premises. But he would leave the door open for Jamal to enter.

As he was leaving, Jamal yelled to his mother, Tishika, "I'm going over to Jimmy's house to play Gaming Gorilla."

"Okay, but don't go into the 'District.' They're gonna be acting a fool at the Capitol and it's not safe."

Jamal said nothing.

"Jamal Weldon Robinson, did you hear what I said?" Tishika shouted.

"Yes, Mom, I heard you. Stay away from the Capitol," Jamal responded.

"No! Stay out of DC! It's not safe!" Tishika said.

"Okay! Love you, Mom!"

"Love you too, son!"

Leaving the house, Jamal made the right turn toward Jimmy's house. He actually walked to his friend's house, which was only four blocks away, but when he got there, he requested an Uber. As soon as Jamal got in the car, he received a text from Jimmy.

"Were you just in front of my house?"

"Yeah, that was me."

"Wassup? Where u headed that u couldn't get an Uber from your house?"

"Moms don't want me to be in DC, but that's where I'm headed. But if anyone contacts you, just say I'm with you… okay?"

"What's going on? DC ain't the place to be, especially wit the shit at the Capitol!"

"I know, but there's something I gotta to do. U got me?"

"I got u!"

"Thnx!"

"Be safe, bruh!"

"Always!"

When the Uber arrived at the Cleveland Park home of the voice on the phone, Jamal quickly got out, went around to the back, and walked down a few concrete stairs, opening the door to the basement in-law unit. Jamal went to the closet and pulled out a small black backpack. Grabbing it with a sense of urgency, Jamal exited the in-law unit calling another Uber. This time, his destination was Capitol Hill. He also sent a cryptic text to the voice he spoke with earlier to say he was leaving.

The Uber driver informed Jamal that Capitol Hill was off-limits.

"How close can you get?"

"I can probably get you near Pennsylvania Avenue."

"That's cool!"

The Uber driver let Jamal off near the Willard Hotel. There were street vendors anticipating the rally, selling "Make America Great Again" caps in droves. Jamal reasoned he would be less conspicuous if he was adorning a MAGA cap, so he quickly purchased one. But as soon as he put it on, he heard a voice screaming, "Yo, bro! Bro! Hold up!"

Jamal saw a large man, who leaned more toward rotund than physically fit, coming toward him. He moved with a brisk pace, which made Jamal lower his backpack, but as the man got closer, Jamal could see the smile on his face.

"Hey, bro! I'm Paul, one of the organizers of this event. So glad you're here! What's your name and where are you from?"

Somewhat shocked by the greeting, Jamal stammered, "My name is Jamal, and I'm from just over the line in Bethesda. Where are you from, Paul?"

"I'm from Waco, Texas," Paul said with great pride. "Jamal, I stopped you because I wanted to welcome you and say that I so appreciate you being here. I wish we had more brothers willing to get off the Democratic

Party plantation and join us to make this country great again!"

"I know what you mean," Jamal replied.

"Listen," Paul said in a muffled tone. "I've been in contact with several congressional offices. All I can say is that this is going to be a shit storm that the Democrats and disloyal Republicans ain't anticipating. Frankly, I would like to hang that son of a bitch vice president myself. We are here to take our country back! We're getting ready to march up to the Capitol... why don't you walk with me? I will be up front as one of the leaders."

Jamal could hardly believe his good fortune. He was being escorted by one of the leaders of the protest, who, undoubtedly, wanted to parade Jamal up front as proof that the movement was antiracist.

With Paul serving as a type of Moses parting the large crowd, he and Jamal made their way toward the front. Some of the protestors looked at Jamal with bewilderment and vitriol. The expressions on their faces did not suggest many in the crowd wished, as Paul claimed, they had "more brothers." In fact, Jamal felt they were looking at him as if there was already one "brother" over the limit.

When they reached the front of the line, Paul and the other protest leaders tried to say something, but the protestors were already engrossed in their own zealous chants, so the only thing left to do was to march to the Capitol.

Marching toward the Capitol to chants of "Save America," Jamal asked Paul, "What did you mean when you said you had been 'in contact with several congressional offices'?"

"I may have said too much, but just be ready when the fireworks start. This socialist takeover bullshit ends today!"

Jamal said nothing. He couldn't believe what he was hearing. But the chatter that he heard online was confirmed by Paul's somewhat obscure declaration. Jamal had deputized himself to be part of the coalition that would prohibit this from happening. As the crowd got closer to the Capitol, they became more boisterous. There were shouts to kill the Speaker of the House, vice president, as well as other members of Congress deemed as traitors.

At approximately 2:00 PM EST, the protestors breached the perimeter of the Capitol. Moments later, some began scaling the walls. With the Senate in session, the vice president was evacuated to a safe location.

A tweet came directly from the president that many of the protestors read: "The vice president didn't have the courage to do what should have been done to protect our country and our Constitution, giving States a chance to certify a corrected set of facts, not the fraudulent or inaccurate ones, which they were asked to previously certify. USA demands the truth!"

This emboldened the rioters to become more aggressive. Jamal moved away from the crowd and reached into his backpack, pulling out the black-matted Glock 19, a semi-automatic handgun. Discarding his MAGA cap, placing it in his backpack, Jamal now adorned an official-looking cap with the words, "United

States Marine Corps."

As Jamal turned, facing him was a short, rail-thin, bespectacled white guy that appeared to be not much older than him.

Holding his press credential, he said, "I'm Ethan Holder, I'm a freelance reporter for the GrioTV, I'm doing some live stream interviews, are you with this group?"

"No," Jamal said. "I am part of a special detail responsible for providing safety for members of Congress and their staff. I'm prepared to place myself in harm's way if called upon, that's why I'm armed so I can protect myself."

"Can you tell us your name?" Holder asked.

"Jamal."

"What's your last name?" Holder asked.

Sternly, Jamal replied, "It's just Jamal!"

Jamal went to the Capitol entrance that protestors were trying to forcibly enter. Reaching into his bag, he pulled out his Glock, firing one shot above his head as he ran toward the barricaded door. One of the protestors wearing a horned fur headdress and war paint in red, white, and blue, shouted, "That nigger's got a gun!" He immediately charged Jamal, who put two bullets center mass. Immediately, he fell dead. Several others charged Jamal—they were brandishing pipes. He shot two of them. One died, the other seriously wounded. Jamal fled the scene.

Police vehicles were just one block away—they remained stationary during the gunfire. Jamal saw them, placed the Glock in his backpack, and walked with his hands up toward the police vehicles. Bystanders called out to the officers that he had just shot people. Preoccupied with the protestors at the Capitol, the police ignored them. They got into their cars and drove past Jamal without stopping him.

Jamal quickly ran off. He removed his Marine Corps cap, replacing it with his MAGA cap. He then stopped only to send a text. Several blocks away was a parked 1998 Toyota Camry with Virginia license plates. Jamal hopped in and the voice that he had communicated with earlier sat in the driver's seat.

"What happened?" the voice asked.

"I think I killed three of them," Jamal said.

"The news reports say two are dead. But that didn't stop them, they've already entered the Capitol," the voice said.

"So, what I did was for nothing," Jamal responded.

"I wouldn't say that," the voice said. "White folks say they're terrorized by *Black Lives Matter*, but it's other white folks who are trying to destroy the shit they say they cherish."

Leaving the gun and backpack in the car, Jamal got out and walked to a nearby Metro station. As he walked through the door, Tishika was sitting on the couch waiting for him.

Without any visible emotion, she said, "I've been watching the news since you left. They say a young black man that fits your description killed two people. But I said, 'That couldn't be Jamal,' because the photo they had was a young man wearing a fucking MAGA cap! And I know my son, Jamal Weldon Robinson, wouldn't be caught dead with a goddamn MAGA cap!"

Impulsively, Jamal reached for the cap, but it was too late, he had forgotten to remove it. With Tishika staring at the bright red cap, the words *Make America Great Again* stood proxy as an admission of guilt.

Holding back tears, Tishika said, "Jamal, you've got to turn yourself in to the police. The rest will be in God's hands."

Jamal agreed.

On the ride to the Bethesda Police Department, Jamal and Tishika said nothing. As they got out of the car, Jamal asked, "Momma, why haven't you asked me why I did it?"

"Because it doesn't matter, son," Tishika said. "All that matters is what will happen going forward. But none of it changes how much I love you."

After Jamal turned himself in to Bethesda police, he was transferred to federal custody. After pleading not guilty to the crimes he was charged with, Judge Horace Banks set Jamal's bail at $2 million. Less than 48 hours after Jamal was charged with fatally shooting two people and wounding a third, famed defense attorney, Clinton Jackson, announced via Twitter he was representing Jamal and his family, and that his client—facing homicide charges—was acting in lawful self-defense. Jackson set up a GoFundMe page that quickly raised the requisite money for bail three times over.

Suddenly, Jamal had become a cause celebre. Liberal historians framed his actions in the context of Crispus Attucks, the black sailor, generally believed to be the first person killed in America's quest for independence against the British Empire in 1770.

Conservatives labeled him a vigilante that killed innocent lives by taking the law into his own hands. They mocked his case for self-defense, noting that nothing prompted him to leave his Bethesda home other than a bloodthirsty desire to kill white people. Newspaper columnists and bloggers queried how could America be so divided.

In the court of public opinion, where legal analysis was freely tossed about without the burden of a law degree, Jamal's fate was rendered well before each side in the actual legal proceedings provided opening remarks. For months, Jamal's case was the fodder for primetime cable talk shows, as his case was prematurely tried and retried by pundits.

One noted legal scholar offered, "If stupidity and implausibility were capital offenses, Robinson's legal defense team would be planning a strategy to spare him from lethal injection. Because neither are crimes, it appears both can be invoked as a viable legal strategy that Robinson's defense team is preparing that will not adversely prejudice the jury against their client."

After posting bail, Jamal's movements were not restricted. However, that was changed after he was spotted at a restaurant with leaders of the local Black Lives Matter chapter. The video captured Jamal as he entered the restaurant being serenaded by a standing ovation from those in attendance. Complete strangers stopped by his table to thank him for his courage. After the video went viral, the conditions for Jamal's bail were modified so that he could only leave his house when accompanied by Tishika.

For as much as Jamal Robinson had become a household name, he was merely a bit player in America's longest-running sequel—its unresolved racial tension. Though America's racial tension has taken on many forms over the centuries, it was the ratification of the Constitution in 1788 that gave the institution of slavery constitutional protection. Since that moment, the nation has been in moral tension with itself. Jamal's actions on Capitol Hill were merely another data point that reminded the nation of that ongoing tension.

The trial began as each side in the court of public opinion had predicted. The prosecution framed Jamal as a vigilante and his defense team, led by Jackson, portrayed him as a patriot protecting the nation that he loved. The most controversial aspect of the trial was the decision to put Jamal on the stand. Under Jackson's tutelage, Jamal was well prepared. Unruffled by the prosecution questions, Jamal stuck to the responses designed by Jackson.

Jackson asked Jamal, "How did you know about the January 6 uprising?"

Jamal responded, "I saw videos on social media, on Facebook live streams and TikTok. I saw the Capitol was the destination of the protestors."

"Why did you take it upon yourself to go to the Capitol?" Jackson asked.

"Because that's the people's house!" Jamal said. Adding, "That house represents everyone, regardless of your race, gender, or sexual orientation. And one group, based on a series of false beliefs, don't have the right to destroy it."

"Jamal," Jackson said. "You were scheduled to join the Marines before the events of January 6 occurred. Is that correct?"

"Yes, sir."

"Jamal, do you know the Marine Corps oath?"

"Yes, sir."

"Would you cite the first two sentences for the jury?"

Looking straight ahead, body erect, Jamal said, "I, Jamal Weldon Robinson, do solemnly swear that I will support and defend the Constitution of the United States against all enemies, foreign and domestic; that I will bear true faith and allegiance to the same."

The body language of several members of the jury suggested they were moved by Jamal's words. Even conservative pundits, who maintained that Jamal was guilty of brazen vigilante justice, confessed to being moved when he cited a portion of the Marine Corps oath.

Looking Jamal directly in the eye, Jackson asked, "Was it your intention to shoot anyone?"

"No, sir."

Would you have shot anyone that was not coming at you?"

"No, sir."

"When one of the protestors said, 'That nigger's got a gun,' were you afraid for your life?"

"Yes, sir."

"Do you recall what happened in the moment that you shot the attackers?"

"Objection!" cried the prosecution. "The defense attorney has no grounds to refer to those shot as 'attackers'."

"How should I refer to them?" Jackson asked smugly.

Jackson's rhetorical question was in response to an earlier ruling by Judge Harrison Barnes, who had replaced Judge Banks, stating that the people Jamal shot could not be referred to as 'victims'.

Reiterating his ruling, Judge Barnes said that referring to those shot as 'victims' could unduly influence the jury, while the use of 'attackers' could be understood in a similar light. In this context, however, it seems to be an accurate description of the individuals in question. It was on this basis that he allowed Jackson's use of the term.

Taking full advantage of the leeway provided by Judge Barnes, Jackson turned back to Jamal, who had apparently become increasingly emotional recalling the moments of January 6, asking, "Tell the court what happened as you were being attacked?"

Jamal's response was interrupted by hyperventilation to the point his words were inaudible. Realizing the critical moment of the testimony, Judge Barnes called for a brief 10-minute recess to give Jamal time to compose himself.

When court resumed, Jamal seemed more composed, recounting the moments that led to him shooting three people with clarity and detail. But as he continued, the emotion returned. Seizing the moment, Jackson asked Jamal, "Is there anything you would like to add?"

Through the emotion-laden stutters, which apparently came without tears, Jamal said, "I didn't do anything wrong! I defended my country and myself!"

Most legal analysts waited with anticipation for Jackson's closing remarks. They were legendary in their ability to get the jury to focus on the essence of Jackson's defense, which may or may not be related to the law in question. But in this case, the federal laws defining self-defense were in alliance with Jackson's rationale.

Jackson, a rather flamboyant character, strode across the courtroom. His dark brown suede loafers were barely audible. What was noticeable was the firm grip he had on the lapels of his white sear sucker suit with baby blue stripes. Jackson had adopted the mannerisms and accouterments of the stereotype held for the southern country lawyer, which belied his east coast education and professional training.

"Ladies and gentlemen of the jury," he said with his booming baritone voice. "Criminal trials are not referendums on politics or social movements. The First Amendment right to free speech or assembly, or our Second Amendment right to bear arms are not on trial. The only message a verdict in a criminal trial sends is that the jury was either convinced of the defendant's guilt beyond a reasonable doubt or it was not. It does not matter how many high-profile individuals speak out one way or the other on what the outcome of this case should be."

Jackson then turned toward Jamal, saying, "The only thing that matters is whether you believe that Jamal

Weldon Robinson violated the federal laws of self-defense as articulated by federal guidelines. How you feel personally and how you would have handled the situation had you been on Capitol Hill on that tragic day of January 6, 2021 are irrelevant. The only thing that matters is that you examine the law and apply those standards to Jamal."

"Did the prosecution prove beyond a reasonable doubt that Jamal violated the law? I am sympathetic to the fact that juries are not a collection of automatons—you have thoughts and feelings. But in this role, you are only permitted to render one of two verdicts: guilty or not guilty. Let me add, by finding Jamal not guilty, you're not saying he is innocent or that his actions were in line with your morality. You are saying, however, that he did not violate the law as it was written. When we think of the events of January 6 in totality, innocence is not among the available choices. For more than two centuries, America has had a peaceful transfer of power. On January 6, that was taken away. Jamal didn't take it away—he was trying to preserve it. If there is a group that is morally blameworthy, it is those that planned the January 6 riots, including the elected officials that, in some capacity, supported it. But none of those cowards are on trial, only my client based not on the subjectivity of morality but the objectivity of the law."

"The prosecution has offered that Jamal's claim that he acted in self-defense is bogus. That argument is based on the following set of suppositions:

The fact he was not legally allowed to possess the gun he used to kill two people and seriously injure a third.

He had no reason to be on Capitol Hill pretending to be some sort of security detail as reported by GrioTV.

Carrying a semi-automatic handgun in public is an act that puts others in fear for their safety, so attempts to disarm him are not a sufficient justification for the use of deadly force.

"I would say all these beliefs are reasonable, but they are beliefs and have nothing to do with federal law. Under the law, Jamal does not relinquish his self-defense claims because he may have been in illegal possession of a firearm. While many people feel that openly carrying a semi-automatic handgun in public is dangerous and invites confrontation, the Supreme Court said in the landmark ruling *DC v. Heller*, under the Second Amendment, individuals have the right to bear arms."

Jackson shrewdly omitted that, under federal law, minors, which Jamal was at the time of the shooting, were not covered under the Second Amendment.

"If you find Jamal's actions morally incomprehensible," Jackson stated calmly. "Then your argument is against those that created the law. But that's not why we're gathered here today. You are not charged with ending a philosophical debate or solving moral conundrums that have been ongoing since the nation's inception. Your sole responsibility is to ascertain whether Jamal acted in accordance with the law. Assuming that is your role, I cannot see how you would reach any verdict other than not guilty. I thank you for your time and indulgence of my soliloquy."

With that, Jackson sat down. He tapped Jamal on his shoulder and then turned to Tishika to offer a look of confidence.

After five days of deliberations, the jury found Jamal "not guilty" on all charges. Half of America that wanted a particular outcome leaped with joy, while the other half bemoaned the outcome as further evidence of an America in decline. The legal community was more aligned. Citing the flexibility in the self-defense laws enacted by Congress as the real culprit, and that the jury had no other choice if they were applying the laws but to find Jamal not guilty.

Cheers went up as Jamal exited the courtroom. Tishika was beside herself with joy as she clung to Jamal's left arm. Suddenly, three shots rang out from within the crowd. All three hit Jamal center mass. He died instantly. A large white man stood over Jamal's body, saying, "Like I said, bro, we're taking our country back."

These were the thoughts Tishika was having as she painfully watched Jamal's body lowered at the graveside funeral ceremony with only a few family members in attendance. The images conjured in Tishika's mind of what *could have been* was the only way she could make sense of the absurdity that was now living in her home rent-free. All she had was a note that Jamal left behind on January 6 that explained what he was doing and the reasons behind his actions. The note concluded with Jamal writing: "Momma, this is something that I must do, please understand! I love you, J."

Jamal Weldon Robinson was not a cause celebre, no one posted his $2 million bail or funded his expensive legal fees. There was no trial. Jamal never killed anyone. He didn't have the opportunity. Jamal had been shot in the head and died instantly on January 6 when a member of the Secret Service sniper team saw him headed toward the Capitol entrance with his Glock exposed. Federal authorities surmised, given Jamal was at the front of the line, he could have been one of the leaders they had yet to identify.

CHAPTER 3

Filth

American politics has always been infiltrated by the extremes that offer strident answers of certainty to issues, which often require nuance. With more than one-fifth of the 21st century having elapsed, it appears certainty has become mainstream in some circles.

Terrance Sanford was the embodiment of certainty. Sanford became Mississippi's first African American governor riding the momentum of moral certainty, as he and his fellow religious conservatives defined it. Can one be morally certain publicly without the sting of hypocrisy privately?

ON NOVEMBER 5TH at approximately 7:05 PM CST, Mississippi Lt. Governor, Terrance Sanford, became governor-elect of the Magnolia State. In doing so, he became Mississippi's first African American governor. Based solely on Sanford's origins, many would conclude his political rise was an improbable story. Sanford stood 5'9 and physically appeared to be in a losing battle with obesity. At 55 years old, his receding hairline and graying temples prematurely aged him by 10 years.

Sanford's career in politics officially began as the mayor of Mound Bayou, Mississippi. He was now headed to the statehouse in Jackson as a firebrand conservative. Though technically a member of the Democrat Party, while mayor of the predominantly African American town of Mound Bayou, Sanford had become the darling of the culture conservatives within the Republican Party for his unabashed stand against homosexuality.

Mound Bayou had never been a large town—the official census in 1900 was 287. Located in the Mississippi Delta, Mound Bayou was a town founded in 1887 by the formerly enslaved. It was designed to be a self-reliant, autonomous, all-black community. For decades, Mound Bayou thrived and prospered, becoming famous for empowering its black citizens. Mound Bayou proudly claims civil rights activists Fannie Lou Hamer and Medgar Evers, among the notables that either lived or worked in the area.

But the town that President Theodore Roosevelt called "The Jewel of the Delta" and Booker T. Washington praised as a model of "thrift and self-government," like so much of the state had fallen on hard economic times. With a population that had dwindled to 1,200 from its 1980 apex of 3000, Mound Bayou became vulnerable to the allure of certainty that Sanford's demagoguery provided.

Growing up in Mound Bayou, Sanford was the seventh of 10 children. He had an abusive father and a mother who struggled with drug abuse until she overdosed when Sanford was 12. From that point, he spent the remainder of his adolescent years in foster care. Upon graduating from high school, Sanford went to work for a nearby hotel, while taking classes at Mississippi Delta College.

It was at Mississippi Delta College that he discovered a love of history, but more importantly, a passion for arguing with his instructors. The subject bore little importance, whichever side it appeared his instructor held, or the one shared by the majority of his classmates, Sanford, regardless of his personal beliefs, would gladly take the contrarian side. His arguments were usually not burdened with the validity the opposing side may have had, nor was Sanford concerned about actually listening. The exhilaration, rooted in Sanford's perceived certainty, transformed every debate into a war of attrition where Sanford was invariably the last person standing. This predictable outcome had more to do with Sanford's unwillingness to acknowledge even the areas where his analysis may have been lacking than the superiority of his debating skill. His fellow students found debating him to not be worth the time. Sanford perfected this skill when he transferred to Mississippi Valley State University—a public historically black university.

It was a history class at Mississippi Valley focused on the civil rights movement of the 1950s and 60s that became a turning point for Sanford. He refused to accept that Bayard Rustin, the lead organizer for the March on Washington for Jobs and Freedom, was openly gay. Sanford based his beliefs on his confidence that, had

Martin Luther King known about Rustin's homosexuality, there would have been no way he would have allowed him to participate in the movement, especially if King were a "Man of God," as he claimed.

Cameron McCoy, Sanford's history professor, assigned the class the following short essay questions for homework:

Was Bayard Rustin openly gay?

If so, did Martin Luther King know about Rustin's homosexuality?

Did King approve of Rustin organizing the March on Washington?

Sanford rushed out of class and headed straight to the library. He salivated at the thought of proving his classmates wrong. He googled: *Was Bayard Rustin gay*? The first story was a Washington Post article that read: "Arrested for having sex with men, this gay civil rights leader could finally be pardoned in California." The article detailed the history, including how Representative Adam Clayton Powell Jr. King blackmailed King that he would spread rumors that he and Rustin were lovers if King did not remove Rustin from the civil rights' inner circle. But it was the other story that left Sanford in disbelief.

In August of 1963, South Carolina Senator, Strom Thurmond, rose on the Senate floor to place a copy of Rustin's 1953 morals charge booking into the Congressional Record, referring to Rustin as 'Mr. March-on-Washington' himself. Because Thurmond's actions were two weeks prior to the march, there was no way, Sanford reasoned, King would not know. Sanford then located an FBI transcript of a conversation between King and an unidentified associate. The associate then said to King: "I hope Bayard don't take a drink before the march." King responded, "Yes, and grab one little brother. Cause he will grab one when he has a drink."

I've been betrayed, Sanford thought to himself. *The civil rights movement depended on some faggots! King ain't shit!*

The next class period found Sanford on time, embracing his usual look of preparedness.

Professor McCoy asked, "Who would like to begin with what they discovered?"

Sanford quickly raised his hand. With the acknowledgement of Professor McCoy, he stated, "I had no idea that what we have been taught is bullshit. We were taught that black people fought for their rights nonviolently, and I discovered the civil rights movement is part of the 'gay agenda.' I see why gays want to link their issues with the civil movement because it's the same thing."

Another student, LaTonya, responded, "Well, it is the same thing in that people's rights were denied."

"It's not the same thing!" Sanford snapped. "You don't see heterosexuals leading gay marches, do you? And you sure as hell don't see men leading marches for women's shit. The only way Rustin could have been a leader in that movement is because it was really about gay rights!"

"You sick for that," LaTonya shouted back.

"I'm just calling it like I see it," Sanford said.

"So, no gay people should have participated in the

civil rights movement?" LaTonya asked.

"That's right," Sanford responded.

"Why? That's so stupid to think that way."

"BECAUSE THAT SHIT IS FILTH!" Sanford shouted.

Realizing he had lost control, Professor McCoy dismissed the class but asked Sanford to stay.

Appearing somewhat contrite, Sanford sat in his seat, and when the last student exited, he said, "Professor McCoy, I'm sorry for shouting, but those are my feelings."

"Terrance, how you feel is your right, but how you express those feelings could be a different matter."

"How so?"

"You just referred to an entire group of human beings as filth. How would you feel if someone in this class, especially someone who was not black, referred to African Americans as filth?"

"That's not the same thing. I can't remove my skin. No one has to know that you're gay unless you tell them."

"The dignity of every person must be affirmed, at least in my class."

"Pastor Dunbar at New Jerusalem Baptist Church teaches that the biblical principles say that homosexuality is wrong, and as Christians, we must stand against it."

"This classroom is not New Jerusalem Baptist Church and I'm not Pastor Dunbar, but you must agree to the class rules, including 'everyone will be treated with dignity and respect.' If you can't do that, this may not be the best class for you."

"Are you kicking me out of the class?"

"No, but I cannot tolerate any more outbursts like today."

Sanford left Professor McCoy's classroom feeling like he had been silenced. He blamed Professor McCoy's stance on the power of the "gay agenda." He told the members at New Jerusalem what happened during Tuesday night Bible study. Pastor Dunbar urged him not to drop the class. Paraphrasing Job 14:14, Pastor Dunbar said, "All the days of your hard service, my son, wait, till your change comes." Pastor Dunbar assured Sanford that the Lord had bigger plans for him that did not include being the loudest voice in a civil rights history course at Mississippi Valley State.

Sanford took the experience at Bible study as a divine affirmation that he was on the path of righteousness and that part of his calling was to stand against what he perceived as the evils of the "gay agenda."

Sanford's political breakthrough came several years later when he was a middle school teacher in Jackson. There was a movement to cancel a gun show that was on the heels of a mass shooting in a St. Louis shopping mall that killed five people. Unrestrained by the guardrails he felt Professor McCoy had established, Sanford unleashed a public diatribe of how the city was attempting to rob him of his divinely inspired Second Amendment rights.

"God gave everything within the garden to defend itself," Sanford said. "He even gave the snails shells to protect themselves from danger. If God would do that much for the snail, how much more would he do for man? God knew that once man left the garden what type of world he would face. He knew the evil that waited. So those AR-15s and Glock 9mms are gifts from the Almighty to defend ourselves the way He gave the snail a shell to defend itself."

Sanford also added that any talk about canceling the gun show was evidence of liberal racism that did not want the black man to arm himself. Sanford's public outcries and media attention cost him his job at the middle school, but quickly gained a following among evangelical conservatives.

They convinced Sanford to return to Mound Bayou and establish it as a political base. They would do the rest in terms of publicity throughout the state, and by creating a job for his wife, Yolandra, so that they would be financially comfortable. Most important, with Mound Bayou being nearly an all-black town, it was decided that Sanford maintained the veneer of being a Democrat, at least for the short term. The decision to remain Democratic was pragmatic and politically cynical.

It was pragmatic in the sense that starting out as a black Republican in a practically all-black constituency that had been traditionally Democratic could present a hurdle too high to overcome, labeling Sanford before he had an opportunity to speak. It was politically cynical because it played on the homophobia that was already present in the black church. Homophobia in the black church was so powerful that congregations overlooked policies championed by Sanford that could be harmful to their communities. When asked about this apparent contradiction on CNN, the Reverend Raphael Lyons of Brooklyn, N.Y. said, "Sanford had successfully proved the emotional attachment to a shared hatred can overcome a multitude of disagreements. It is a classic and unfortunate real-life example of the proverb: 'The enemy of my enemy is my friend'."

Sanford built a base of support within evangelical churches. Though his initial support was in the Mound Bayou area, with the help of his backers, he was speaking throughout the state of Mississippi against the wages of sin. Sanford bemoaned how the church had lost its way and how the "gay agenda" had coopted the civil rights movement and now had its grip on the church.

"Inclusivity," Sanford would shout. "As the world defines it, will be the end of the church. And that's one of the goals of the gay agenda."

As his popularity grew, Sanford became increasingly focused on his opposition to homosexuality. It seemed that's all he wanted to discuss, which was perfectly acceptable to his evangelical base because that was all they wanted to hear.

When he announced that he was a candidate for the Republican nomination for Lt. Governor. His support among evangelicals, coupled with the crossover vote he would receive from black voters that traditionally vote Democratic, made him formidable. As mayor of Mound Bayou, Sanford had not given much thought to serious public policy. As a Republican, Sanford accepted the party's traditional positions on tax cuts and abortion.

Sanford won a tight primary race, but won the election handily. He was reelected four years later. After Sanford's reelection, talk, which was instigated by his advance team, began touting him as the next governor.

Sanford garnered national headlines when he traveled to Raleigh, North Carolina to lend his support for the "Bathroom Bill." The "Bathroom Bill" was the common name for the legislation passed by the North Carolina Republican-led state legislature over the veto of the state's Republican governor that defined access to public toilets based on the assigned sex at birth.

Standing on the steps of the state Capitol in Raleigh surrounded by thousands of supporters, detractors, and cameras, Sanford declared, "There ain't but two genders, ain't nothing but men and women. I don't understand this unisex stuff. Don't no woman want to be using the bathroom next to a man. How can you explain that to your children? You can't! How can you explain it to God? You can't!"

To a thunderous ovation, mocking the words of comedian, Chris Rock, Sanford boastfully chanted, "Yeah, I said it!"

"There's no reason to be telling any child in America about transgenderism, homosexuality... any of that filth," he told the audience. "And yes, I called it filth!"

These statements, deplorable to some, yet hailed by others, allowed Sanford to raise money outside the state, swelling his campaign coffers and becoming the most recognizable name in the state. He dubbed every criticism levied toward him as a critique against those who supported him. With the use of social media,

Sanford became Willie Stark from the 1946 novel, *All the King's Men*, updated for the 21st century.

From that point, every speech Sanford gave, in some manner, provided a reference to his antipathy for the LGBTQ community, and how their goals were a threat to society. "What purpose does homosexuality serve? What does it make? What does it create? It creates nothing," he told the New Jerusalem congregation who celebrated his return.

He justified that any inequality sustained by the LGBTQ community was a result of the subordinate position they held in society. Sanford would routinely tell crowds that a gay man asked him, "So, you think your heterosexual relationship is superior to my husband and my homosexual relationship?"

"Yes!" Sanford bellowed to the congregation. "Heterosexuals are superior because we can do something those people can't do. Because that's the way God created it. And I'm tired of this society trying to tell me it ain't so."

Sanford went on to challenge the validity of Martin Luther King as a social activist. He told white evangelicals that King knew Bayard Rustin was a "sissy" and did nothing about it. He then rhetorically asked the congregation, "If you call yourself a man of God, but have homosexuals in your midst, you know they are homosexuals and you don't do anything about it… first, you ain't no man of God. Second, there is only one reason that I can think of that you won't do something about it. We need to think real hard about the continuation of this charade, giving Martin Luther King a holiday in the name of civil rights when it's really the gay agenda at work."

When asked by a reporter about his divisive tone, Sanford shot back, "It's divisive to those that hate God and want to tear down everything that America stands for. Whereas I want to preserve everything that the country stands for."

Once Sanford secured his party's gubernatorial nomination, the outcome was never in doubt. In Mississippi, a glass of ice water with the words "Republican" taped on, would win decisively over the state's most popular Democrat. That's why CNN was able to call the race minutes after the polls closed. The moment the race was called, Sanford hugged Yolandra. It was a passionate embrace that embodied his growing up in Mound Bayou, through Mississippi Valley State, to his time as Mound Bayou's mayor to the moment he was declared Mississippi's next governor. Some political pundits condemned Sanford's approach; others pointed out how that "political approach" garnered 53% of the vote. They noted that however one feels about Sanford, some 400,000 voters in some measure feel as he does.

At approximately 9:00 CST, Mississippi's former governor, Winthrop Haskins, came to the podium. At 86, Haskins was still a beloved figure within the state.

"Ladies and gentlemen, we did something tonight that the prognosticators said couldn't be done—that our party was too racist. And that woman who, in my view, has been infected with a malignant case of insanity, who writes for the New York Times, used the words of that song Strange Fruit as a depiction of Mississippi today. It was a despicable display of journalism, if you ask me. Now we do have a legacy, here in Mississippi, that we're not proud of, but we showed the country tonight what can happen when a state is willing to learn from its past. It is my pleasure and esteemed honor to present to you Mississippi's next governor, the man you're sending to Jackson, The Honorable Terrance L. Sanford!"

What was once impossible had transformed into reality. Terrence Sanford was the Governor-elect of Mississippi. With Yolandra at his side, Sanford soaked in the adulation. He opened by saying, "Not bad for a little ole black kid from Mound Bayou!"

The crowd roared.

"They said Mississippi would never elect a black man as its governor. They said my positions were too radical. They said that I was trying to take Mississippi back to the Stone Ages."

Taking a slight moment to pause, Sanford said, "Now I don't know how you get on that 'They Committee', but let me tell you what those on that "They Committee" didn't know. Mississippi did elect a black governor, Mississippians did not think my positions were too radical, and Mississippians did not believe I was trying to take them back to the Stone Ages because they know the only place where the Stone Ages existed was on the Flintstones. Mississippians know our destination is the land of milk and honey."

Once again, the crowd roared enthusiastically.

"There are too many people to thank for my being here," Sanford said. "But there are two I must acknowledge. First, my queen, the wind beneath my wings, my lovely wife, Yolandra, who is going to make a great first lady by making all Mississippians proud. I would like to also thank my campaign manager, Dick Sargent, who kept me on task and was the brainchild behind this historic victory."

"Let me say one more thing. It's a new day in Mississippi—a day when we take the state back to the way things ought to be. Our doors are open to anyone willing to work hard and play by the rules. But if you just want to sit and have the government take care of you, I'm here to tell you, you're in for a rude awakening. This is a state, under my leadership, where the only "PC" we will adhere to are the products not made by Apple! We don't need to be woke... we're already woke—woke to the fact that God only made two genders. And that's not going to change as long as I'm governor of Mississippi. Thank you for this honor! Goodnight! God Bless you, and may God bless the great state of Mississippi."

Walking off the stage with Yolandra at his side, the crowd in the ballroom was at a feverish pitch. Evangelicals had their man who stood for their values. The gun lobby had their man who stood for their issues. And the business community had their man who didn't give much thought to their issues, but would do whatever they suggested.

People crowded around Sanford for selfies and impromptu lobbying efforts, causing him to become separated from Yolandra. Sanford was a hot commodity, at least in the state of Mississippi, he didn't notice Yolandra was no longer at his side. Like pigs at the feeding trough, Sanford consumed the adoration. But he was also a divisive figure whose vision extended only as far as those that supported his agenda. As far as Sanford was concerned, he was elected to serve those that voted for him. He had no regard for the opposition, which he saw as equivalent to the locust plague articulated in the Book of Exodus. With the crowd surrounding Sanford, Yolandra had trouble making her way back to him. With the assistance of Dick Sargent, who aggressively elbowed his way through the crowd, creating a pathway for Yolandra, she tugged her husband by the arm and said, "Terrance, I'm headed to the room. How much longer do you think you will be down here?"

"Dick just told me a few minutes ago there's a short meeting with some funders that I must attend."

"I was going to ask if I should wait up… so we could really celebrate your victory."

"What did you have in mind?" Sanford asked.

"I was thinking about having you lay hands on me along with talking in tongues, if you know what I mean?" Yolandra said slyly.

"Why, Mrs. Sanford, you got a dirty mind, I'm happy to say," Sanford said in a coy manner.

"But I also know about you and them damn funders," she quickly lamented. "You're not even officially the governor yet and they already want their pound of flesh. So, I'm not going to wait up!"

"So says the next first lady of the great state of Mississippi," Sanford said in a flirtatious manner.

With that, Yolandra kissed Sanford and walked away beaming.

Dick walked up, already two drinks beyond his limit.

"Governor! Oh, I like the sound of that!" he said with an inebriated grin. "Are you ready to head up?"

"Wait a second. Let Yolandra get up to the room."

Sanford and Dick left the victory party. They took the elevator up to the suite where Dick bid Sanford adieu. As Sanford got off the elevator, he held the door, "Remember, if you happen to run into Yolandra, I'm having sensitive talks with donors that you were not allowed to be privy to."

Dick just smiled as the door closed.

Thirty minutes later, there was a knock on the door of the suite. Sanford, dressed in only a hotel robe, patent leather pumps with six-inch heels, ruby red lipstick, and a blonde wig, answered the door. Sanford was holding a martini in his right hand, which ran counter to the "Christian" image he promoted as one that abstained from alcohol. Two physically fit men entered—one black, the other white, both in their late 20s and well endowed, all per Sanford's request to the agency.

"You boys ever fuck a governor before?" Sanford asked as the two men undressed in the middle of the suite. Leading them into the bedroom, Sanford took off his robe, and with his nude flabby body, got on the bed on all fours. With one escort in the front and the other in the back, he said, "You bitches know what I want."

After the escorts left, Sanford sat in the corner of the bedroom crying—it was part of his self-flagellation routine that always followed his sexual encounters with men. As the tears flowed, riddled with guilt and shame,

Sanford tried to convince himself he was not gay—a process that was successful until he was overcome by his sexual desires for a return engagement.

As he was about to leave the suite, he noticed that one of the escorts had left a black satin thong on the floor. Sanford quickly walked over, picked it up, and mumbled to himself, "Fucking faggots!"

CHAPTER 4

Woke

Woke is the 21st-century term defined as being alert to social and/or racial discrimination and injustice. But does being "woke" equate to being right? In the age of "wokeness", is there a corresponding role for circumspection and critical thinking? Or is it profoundly American in its susceptibility to the vices of certainty?

THERE WAS A FIRM knock on the door. Claire Levinson, the dean of the Middlebrook University School of Law, assumed it was George Hatfield as she was expecting him.

For more than 20 years, Hatfield's constitutional law classes made him one of the most popular instructors at the institution. He was lauded for his ability to make the Constitution alive and relevant. He was a go-to interviewee for many of the cable news shows when there was a constitutional question dominating public discourse.

"Come in."

"Hey, Claire," George said in a jovial tone—the

remnants from the exuberance he usually experienced immediately after his class concluded.

"Hello, George."

"You know, it was rather serendipitous to get your text about stopping by your office after class because Jeannie and I wanted to have you and Bill over for dinner, and now when Jeannie asks if I have spoken with you, I can answer in the affirmative."

"Oh, that would be lovely, I'm sure Bill will welcome it as well. I'll text him now. We should talk about some possible dates, but first, there's something else I need to discuss with you."

"Sure, what's up?"

"We received several reports from students that you made racist comments in class," Claire said.

"What?" George said in disbelief.

George had spent a lifetime—or so he thought—proving his solidarity with those on the underside of life. He served as statewide executive director of the ACLU, and was a fervent believer that society must err on the side of protecting the civil liberties of its citizens. In George's law school office was a quote that hung on the wall, a gift from his ACLU staff that read: "Constitutional protection, like Mathew 5:45, rains on the just and the unjust." George was proud of that quote. He originated it while defending the Ku Klux Klan's right to march through a local community. It encapsulated what he believed was the nation's constitutional inheritance.

George grew up during the presidency of Dwight Eisenhower. He felt his idyllic upbringing was best captured by 1950s sitcom, Leave It to Beaver. His mother, like June Cleaver, did not work outside the home and benefitted from the services of a Negro domestic whose name was Matilda.

Matilda was a surrogate mother to George and his sister. She made the best grits he ever tasted. It was also the only grits he had ever tasted until he became an adult, but Matilda's still reigned supreme.

His father, unlike Ward Cleaver whose actual job was unclear, was a powerful corporate attorney. As long as George could remember, all he ever wanted to be was an attorney. But any desires he held to follow exactly in his father's footsteps were permanently altered by the events of February 1, 1960 in Greensboro, NC.

The televised news coverage of the nonviolent sit-in movement to desegregate a lunch counter, led by four students from North Carolina A&T, galvanized a community of young whites, as well as Negroes, to put an end to racial segregation. George recalled his father seemed dismissively ambivalent on an issue he was a passionate supporter of.

"The Negroes have a constitutional point," he remarked to George. But he also understood the resistance because he added, "After all, we are talking about Negroes."

George seldom disagreed with his father, certainly not publicly. Selectively ignoring the second part of his father's remarks, what George heard was that the Negroes "have a constitutional point." He made up his mind that he would commit his life to protecting those with a constitutional point.

George joined the local chapter of the NAACP, attended the 1963 March on Washington for Jobs and Freedom with a local church congregation, and was upset that local NAACP officials deemed him too young to participate in the 1965 march from Selma to Montgomery, Alabama. He cried uncontrollably when he learned that civil rights workers had been murdered in Philadelphia, Mississippi in 1964. Those emotions returned when he stayed home from school to watch the funeral of Dr. Martin Luther King, Jr. in 1968.

George attended Harvard University undergrad and law school, and clerked for Supreme Court Justice Thurgood Marshall before going to work at the ACLU. He had known Claire for many years—she recruited him to join the law school faculty. It was a difficult decision to leave the ACLU as George assumed he would retire there, representing those with a constitutional point. But Claire convinced him by quoting his own words:

"If the Constitution does not make you side with someone or something that you fervently disagree with in your soul, then you haven't considered its paradoxical and radical implications." Claire told George that type of pedagogical approach was sorely needed at Middlebrook.

But now, seated in front of his colleague and personal friend, who had known him and his wife, Jeannie, for more than a quarter of a century, levied charges of racism in his direction.

"I suppose you can't tell me who said it?"

"No, but I can tell you it was more than one person."

Perplexed, George responded, "I don't know what to say other than it's simply not true."

"More than half your Constitutional Law I class has come to me in some manner to say you used the "N-word" multiple times.

"WHAT?" George cried out in frustration.

Then he paused. There was one occasion that he did use the infamous "N-word" but surely that could not be the reason...

No fucking way, he thought to himself.

"Claire, what exactly did they accuse me of?"

"As far as I can tell," Claire said, now sounding somewhat reluctant. "The students took issue that you used the word during your discussion of *Brandenburg v. Ohio.*"

George's seemingly preposterous supposition seconds ago had been confirmed. He was accused of racism because he had read the speech contained in the con law footnotes of *Brandenburg v. Ohio*—a seminal First Amendment case taught at practically every accredited law school in the nation.

In 1964, Clarence Brandenburg was an Ohio Ku Klux Klan leader who gave inflammatory speeches, denigrating certain ethnicities, peppered with racial epithets, including the liberal use of "nigger." Brandenburg suggested in his speeches the possibility of violence against certain groups. He was charged with violating Ohio's Criminal Syndicalism law, which made it a crime to "advocate ... the duty, necessity, or propriety of crime, sabotage, or unlawful methods of terrorism." He was fined and sentenced to serve one to 10 years in prison.

In 1969, the Supreme Court unanimously ruled (8-0) that the government could not punish inflammatory speech unless that speech is "directed to inciting or producing imminent lawless action and is likely to incite or produce such action."

George had long made it a habit to read Brandenburg's remarks contained in the footnotes. He had read the footnotes in so many of his con law classes that it felt like second nature. Showing no discomfort, he read Brandenburg's words verbatim:

"How far is the nigger going," George read. In another passage, he read, "This is what we are going to do to the niggers."

He continued to read as his class listened uncomfortably to Brandenburg's inflammatory speech: "A dirty nigger. Send the Jews back to Israel. Save America. Let's go back to constitutional betterment. Bury the niggers. Give us our state rights. Freedom for the whites, the nigger will have to fight for every inch he gets from now on."

Though reading Brandenburg's words may have been second nature for George, his class sat silent, eerily looking at each other, stunned at what they just heard. More than the provocative words, they were shocked that one of the most popular instructors at the law school appeared to have no apprehension in reading Brandenburg's words, making George an unindicted co-conspirator, a de facto racist. Oblivious to what had transpired, George dismissed class, sauntering out with his normal exuberance. But the students remained.

They huddled in support of the three African American students in the class, who, like most of their classmates, were bewildered as to why George would repeat those inflammatory words without any forewarning.

"What kind of racist bullshit was that?" one of the students cried out after George left the room.

Looking at the African American students, another student added, "And he didn't give a shit that he was making some of the students extremely uncomfortable. We can't let this shit pass, we should all go to Dean Levinson immediately."

The student's suggestion garnered unanimous support evidenced by the number of emails Claire received, including students that were not enrolled in George's class.

The delightful atmosphere that George greeted Claire with when he entered her office had become solemn.

"George," Claire said. "I can't ignore this. I've got to do something."

"Do something?" George asked. "Judging by your tone, it sounds like you already know what that "something" is. Let me guess… you are going to make me the sacrificial lamb, rather than make those sniveling self-righteous spoiled children grow up."

"I wouldn't put it like that," Claire said.

"I would or we wouldn't be having this conversation."

"George, you should have at least prepared them that the word will be used, allowing those who wish to excuse themselves to do so."

"That's a great suggestion, Claire, because that's how it will work when they leave here and join reality."

"There's no need for sarcasm," Claire snapped.

"I did prepare them, I told them Clarence Brandenburg was a television repairman and a leader of the Klan. As to emphasize the length that the Court was willing to go to protect speech, I also informed them that the unanimous ruling for Brandenburg included Justice Marshall, the first African American on the Court. Can I also assume that my having clerked for Marshall is not factored in the "something" that you must do?"

"According to the Black Student Union, all you said was some, and I'm quoting here, 'liberal white woman' was the lead attorney."

"That's ridiculous... unless of course, Eleanor Holmes Norton, who was the lead council in *Brandenburg*, had a race change that I was unaware of. But when she worked at the ACLU, before she became the U.S. Delegate representing the District of Columbia, she was black."

"George, I get it, but this is a different time," Claire said.

"Are the values and customs so different that truth and critical thinking do not matter?"

"Did you have to say the N-word?"

"Claire, what does the N-word mean?"

"C'mon, George, the history alone makes it the most offensive word in the English language."

"I know that, but right now, I'm asking about the definition."

"I'm not sure I can give you a concise definition," Claire said.

"It doesn't have a definitive meaning," George shot back. "It is an explosive word with no real definition—the only power it has is what society provides. But whatever it means, it's not the same in the mouths of vehement racists or the rappers that use it. I don't understand kowtowing to a group that can use nuance when it benefits them, but hides behind the tenderness of their feelings when it's something they don't like, or in this case, don't understand."

"Well, I have written a statement that will go out this evening."

Claire reached into the main drawer of her desk and pulled out a single sheet of paper, handing it to George. It read:

"A number of students reached out to my office about Professor George Hatfield's use of the "N-word" when teaching *Brandenburg v. Ohio* in Constitutional Law I.

"For the students attending that class, you have my most sincere, heartfelt apology for the pain Professor Hatfield caused many of you when he read aloud the racist footnotes in Brandenburg, which included the most offensive word in the American language—the N-word. Confronting America's discriminatory past through case law can be challenging enough without hearing your professor read that word aloud in a class.

"I also want to offer an apology for students who learned about the incident and were also hurt. Words matter and the consequences of words (not just the intentions behind words) matter. I want to reaffirm my commitment to your learning in a diverse, inclusive, and equitable learning environment. At Middlebrook School of Law, diversity—the mix of different perspectives and experiences that make up a healthy, stimulating classroom—is of paramount importance. Our community shares a tradition that embraces freedom and integrity, acknowledges the worth of the individual, and promotes a democratic spirit arising from open-mindedness and discourse. We failed to carry out that tradition. Together going forward, I want to minimize our failures."

Gazing disappointedly at Claire and then back at the statement, George asked, "What do you think this accomplishes?

"It tells the students they've been heard."

"It tells the students they are being rewarded for having their head up their ass!"

"That's unfair!"

"What's unfair is you offering an apology to students who were not present. Their delicate feelings were damaged by hearsay. What's unfair is that everything I've done throughout my professional life has been ignored by a bunch of no-nothing brats so I can be classified as a fucking racist."

"I don't think you understand the importance of the 'woke' culture."

"I appreciate its importance and how they have expanded the notion of social inequality beyond race, to include issues regarding gender and sexual orientation. I would add throughout the American narrative, there have been those, albeit not identical, that have been 'woke.' That's how the country was formed. It was how slavery was eliminated and women's suffrage passed. Was not my generation 'woke' to the issues of civil rights and Vietnam? But there is a difference between being woke because you are an advocate for change and being woke because you were asleep when they were passing out critical thinking and nuance."

"Doesn't sound as if you much respect their opinions."

"Here's what I know about being woke that falls into the same trap as those that came before it— certainty. The tendency to be certain can rob one of self-reflection, making it difficult to hear the validity of the contrarian perspective. Moreover, once you are certain, you're irrepressibly headed down the road that leads to ignorance. If you send that statement, you're aiding and abetting their unexamined crusade."

"What was acceptable speech when you were in law school is not acceptable today."

"Claire, I think you're overreacting. We're not talking about my words, but the words that led to the most important First Amendment case of the 20th century; it's still the standard. This response sounds as if I was just short of reading Brandenburg's words in blackface while playing a banjo."

"But your words made the students feel unsafe, and if I don't do something, they will also feel that they were not heard."

"We're talking about a word, yes, a horrible word that appears in more than 10,000 court cases, but I'm not allowed to quote it?"

"Part of the students' discomfort was that you apparently appeared comfortable saying it."

"They were not my words... or does that not count for anything?"

"But you read them."

Had I read the Gettysburg Address, do I get to claim ownership?"

"George, I think you know what I mean."

"Claire, vaunted claims of superiority, notwithstanding; are we not part of a university culture that believes we have a moral obligation to present the world as it is? What better way to understand the paradoxical nature of the Constitution than to illustrate that it protects vile speech like that of Brandenburg?"

"Did you have to read the word multiple times?"

"Yes, I did! There is no better example than by showing, which includes actually hearing the words. The Constitution even protects the worst word in the English language. But this conversation is emblematic of a much larger problem."

"How so?"

"You're willing to placate the feelings of those unable to make the connection between the neutrality of speech and that in a democratic society there can never be a choice between the government deciding who can speak and granting the benefit of the doubt to unpopular speech. Unpopular speech is the barometer that measures civil liberty."

"So, how would you handle it?"

"This is a teachable moment—an opportunity to

reaffirm our commitment to education and that we are not a sanctuary for comfort but stand on the vanguard of exploring our thoughts, having our assumptions challenged, even acknowledging that those who see the world differently potentially hold the keys to our enlightenment."

"George, you seem oblivious to the hurt feelings of students."

"It's not that. I'm disappointed that you didn't bother to ask the clarifying question: 'Why did Professor Hatfield reading the words from Brandenburg hurt you?'"

"Why would that matter?"

"It matters because that was the only way you could have found out, as my surrogate mother, Matilda, used to say: "What they mad about ain't what they about. If they can't tell you why they are upset, then it's bullshit!"

Feeling the tension rise, Claire took a deep breath, saying, "I also asked the chair of our faculty Diversity & Inclusion Committee, and the dean for Academic Affairs, to work with students and faculty to submit proposals to me about the next steps."

"My God, we're so far removed from the issue," George lamented.

"What's the issue in your view?"

"Well, it started with eroding the importance of what I consider the most important First Amendment decision rendered by the Supreme Court, but I see that it's now about the law school covering its ass, afraid of its own shadow."

"The importance of Brandenburg can be realized

without reading his words."

"I disagree. The First Amendment is the most important in the Bill of Rights. Without it, there is no civil rights movement or women's suffrage. The Vietnam protest could have been shut down. It is the gateway to advocacy. The feelings of the students you seem so committed to protecting are unable to see that the protection of Brandenburg and his many utterances of "nigger" also protects the valor of the civil right movement. It's possible to say that without quoting Brandenburg, but I don't think the magnitude of the message is the same."

"Doesn't the integrity of the law school matter?"

"If it's the integrity of the law school you're worried about, don't blame the students. This is a farce to appear you're taking action when you're actually making the situation worse. It is you and your cohorts within the administration that threatens the integrity of the law school."

"The law school cannot take a laissez-faire attitude about such matters."

"That sounds nice, but you're just pretending to do something without really doing anything. I would like to know directly from students why reading Brandenburg's words hurt so deeply. You're depriving me of that opportunity."

"We've already agreed this is the best way to handle it."

"By 'we', I'm assuming you mean the university president."

"Yes, that's correct."

"So, this has been one big farce. You had already decided what you were going to do before sending me that text."

"George, I'm sorry but you have to appreciate the situation I'm in."

"Don't you mean the paranoia that the university is under?"

"Several years ago, we probably wouldn't be having this conversation, but we're in a Black Lives Matter moment, so things are different."

"There's always been a Black Lives Matter moment, it's just the country never seems to get around to discussing it authentically, including the present moment. Surely, you're not suggesting my reading Brandenburg's words somehow puts these students on a trajectory toward becoming the next George Floyd, Breonna Taylor, or Philando Castile?"

"Not exactly."

"Not exactly? Each student in this law school represents roughly $50,000 of annual tuition. Their desire to be in literal solidarity with those on the underside of life is, in a word, insufferable," George said.

"Many of those students receive some portion of aid. Middlebrook is not a destination spot for trust fund babies," Claire said.

"No, but you're on the cusp of being the law school where the inmates can freely run the asylum," he responded.

"Are you suggesting the students that attend this law school don't have valid concerns?"

"Of course they do, but my reading Brandenburg

from a college lectern is not among them. Breonna Taylor was a medical technician, Philando Castile was a cook, and George Floyd was believed to be a rapper and security guard. How many students are we grooming to fill those positions?"

"What's that have to do with anything?"

"It has everything to do with it because as far as I can tell, very few of our students take jobs that place them on the front lines, protecting civil liberties. The aggrieved bullshit of the privilege will last until they get their diploma, then most will be headed out the door with delusions of becoming a partner in a prestigious law firm."

"Not all of our students feel that way."

"But enough to make my statement the standard rather than the exception. I'm glad students were uncomfortable at my reading the footnotes in *Brandenburg*. I teach it like that intentionally. I'm raising critical questions. How bad are you committed to the First Amendment? Is it reserved only for the speech you like? Or do you recognize that it's the speech you abhor that protects your speech?"

"Maybe it's time to rethink how you teach *Brandenburg*."

Do you know how long I've been teaching *Brandenburg*? I've always taught it this way."

"I know, George. Maybe that's the problem."

"What the hell does that mean?"

"It means the way you teach *Brandenburg* may no longer be the best way for our students to embrace its value."

Sarcastically, George responded, "I could add an intro to the political science precursor since they all thought Eleanor Holmes Norton was a white liberal do-gooder, which is probably how they see me."

Unwilling to respond to the latter part of George's statement, Claire simply said, "I do know they see you as out of touch, and it's not just *Brandenburg*."

"I'm listening."

"There have been a number of complaints that your resistance to technology, especially during the pandemic, made the learning experience difficult."

"Zoom is creepy! It's like inviting COINTELPRO to the meeting."

COINTELPRO was an abbreviation for Counter Intelligence Program, a covert FBI program used to disrupt American political organizations such as the civil rights movement of the 1950s and 60s and the anti-Vietnam protests—something that George was acutely sensitive about.

"Zoom may be creepy," Claire said. "But it's all we had when we were shut down during the pandemic. And students found it off-putting that you were muted on the video, forced to call in, leaving the video on, creating an echo while you lectured."

"Why am I just now hearing about this? And if this was such a concern, why didn't one of the spoiled children masquerading as law students bring it to my attention?"

"George, you're resistant to email, and you have intimidated all of your teaching assistants. I suspect they have been reluctant to bring it up."

"What are you suggesting?"

Claire took another deep breath because they reached the point of the meeting she was hoping to avoid, had George said anything that she could take back to the school administration to reassure them that he understood the magnitude of the problem. But he would not. Perhaps more pointedly, he could not.

"You've had a great run," she said. "Your presence has made Middlebrook a better institution. I don't want these accusations to be what people remember."

Now it was George's turn to take a deep breath. He asked, "How should we proceed?"

"I think you should put out a statement of apology, craft it however you want, give it several days, and announce your retirement at the end of the school year. Give any reason you want. I was thinking that we should also look into endowing a First Amendment lecture series that bears your name."

"I don't want to sound ungrateful, but might such a series draw the ire of those that already feel unheard?" he said.

"Maybe, but by the time we get the lecture series endowed and planned for the inaugural event, many of them will be gone."

"I hadn't begun contemplating retirement. I convinced myself that I still had something to offer."

"You do," Claire said emphatically. "But it seems that you've lost the one thing crucial to being an effective teacher... and once you lose it, it's difficult to reclaim."

"What's that?"

"Trust."

"Well, it seems you got it all planned out. I don't think there's anything left for me to say. I better get going, it seems I have several swords to fall on."

Slowly getting out of the chair, George turned toward his colleague and friend with a forced smile, "Goodbye, Claire."

"Goodbye, George. We'll talk in a few days?"

"Sounds good."

As George was leaving Claire's office, she stopped him with an enthusiasm that belied their conversation. "I just heard back from Bill, he said, 'How about next Thursday?'"

"Next Thursday is fine, I will tell Jeannie," George said.

"We're looking forward to it."

"So is Jeannie."

CHAPTER 5

Death Row

Though it has lost some of its momentum, the death penalty is still administered in a number of states, placing the United States along with countries such as China, Pakistan, and Saudi Arabia that maintain capital punishment.

Rarely, if ever, do proponents of the death penalty consider that, as a public policy, support must include the acceptance of an error percentage—the possibility that an innocent person might be put to death by the state.

THAT'S PROBABLY THE last time I will ever do that. Who am I kidding? That will be the last time I do that. It's a strange feeling to wake up knowing this day will be my last.

I think it's a new day. I really don't know. The lights are always on and I don't have a window to look out, so I'm depending on my body to tell me what time it is. I still have to knock out my 500 pushups for the day— some things don't change, even if it is my last. Good thing I finished reading *The Count of Monte Cristo* yesterday. There's an organization called *Books on the*

Inside that sends me books each month, so I'm one of the best-read mothafuckas here. I think I've read more than 400 books since I've been here. I don't think I will start another. Maybe there's some shit in the Bible I can look at later today. That seems appropriate. I have spent two decades reading and reflecting, trying to understand how I got here. Reading has been the only thing that has kept me clothed and in my right mind.

One of those Christian Bible belt mothafuckas drops by from time to time telling me about predestination— somehow, this shit was God's will. I'm not a biblical scholar but predestination seems to be some trial-and-error bullshit that someone made up to justify what they don't understand. It's unclear to me why God would have predestined me to this. I'm no prophet. I can't turn water into wine. All I have is the ability to be given a death sentence without committing a crime. But that ain't no miracle—any poor *son of a bitch* who's dumb enough to get caught up in the system can pull it off.

It's easy to talk that predestination shit, especially when your ass ain't on death row. It's even easier to talk about predestination when you believe, as did the district attorney, the judge, the jury of my so-called peers, and even my jackleg public defender that I wasn't fit to live. As in biblical days, I am the fuckin' lamb they slaughter to give the victim's family a sense of justice. Whenever they make the crime about justice for the victim's family, somebody has got to pay. And the family is willing to go along with the charade because they truly believe justice will somehow come out of this shit. But there ain't no justice in this shit—nowhere. The system ain't about justice, and if you believe that, you a new fool!

I looked up justice in the dictionary and it defines it as: "The maintenance or administration of what is just, especially by the impartial adjustment of conflicting claims or the assignment of merited rewards or punishments."

I understood justice less after reading that definition. What I do know is that justice ain't got shit to do with what's fair. Fair, as my grand momma used to say, "Is where you get cotton candy and corn dogs, it don't apply to life."

I hear it takes seven minutes to die after you've been injected. So, after 20 years on death row and an additional seven minutes for my heart to stop, the family of the victim, well, what remains because I suspect some have died, will get their justice. I hope they will get justice because that's some cold shit to tell somebody, only to find out after the fact it ain't true.

I've had time to consider what the family will do with that justice if they get it… will they frame it? Was it worth the 20 years and seven minutes to wait? Or will they wake up tomorrow, just as I did today, and just say, "*What the fuck*?" I sure hope not, but that's probably what will happen. This has to make sense for someone, but I know it won't. That district attorney who looked me in the face and called me an animal that wasn't fit to live during his closing remarks knows it won't. As he stood there with the victim's family, it was as if he had one arm around them as they grieved and the other holding a reelection sign.

As far as I can tell, the death penalty only makes sense to those with no skin in the game. Government that talks about justice for the victim's family members, jurors who feel it's their appointed duty to see that justice prevails, the public defender who held my life in his hands but couldn't remember my name, even those Christian do-gooders that prayed for my soul and left scripture through the slot on my cell door had no skin in the game. It's like being a football fan.

They have the privilege of watching, like the big shots that sit up in those luxury box seats at the Dallas Cowboy games. I hear they pay Jerry Jones damn near $50,000 to sit in those leather chairs with a drink in their hand, wondering, "Why didn't that *mothafucka* block?" But they're not on the field. Those that call for justice ain't on the field. Those that say killing me will stop others from killing are not on the fucking field. Hell, I wasn't even on the field—I was asleep in my bed 10 miles from where the murder occurred. But now I'm here without a murder weapon, motive, or DNA evidence linking my ass to the victim. I didn't have one of those goddamn corroborating witnesses to say I was where I said I was, just that irrefutable testimony that said I "fit the description." To have found me guilty was cruel, but to give me a death sentence was not unusual, so I guess there is no violation of the Eighth Amendment against cruel "and" unusual punishment because I know I ain't the only mothafucka in this situation. But that's some bullshit rationalization because I'm the only mothafucka in this cell that's going to die tonight for no reason.

Mrs. Morgenthau, a short little silver-haired elderly white woman, whose only interaction with people who ain't white is probably to pay them after they do some shit around her house. She told the district attorney she saw someone running from the house where the murder took place. She was the main one that placed me at the scene. Two days after the crime, she saw me running downtown trying to catch a bus, put two and two together, and came up with five. Then others said they saw me in the area near the time of the crime. Suddenly, that "someone" Mrs. Morgenthau saw running from the house became me, who became a person of interest, then a suspect, a target, and finally, guilty of a first-degree murder that qualified for the death penalty.

And some people still think the death penalty is morally right, some of that Old Testament eye for an eye shit. During my trial, some mothafuckas was outside praying, hoping they killed my ass, holding signs that read: "The Punishment Must be Equal to the Crime." That means if someone kills somebody, then the state can kill them. That's like saying, "If someone is guilty of rape, the state can rape them." That shit don't make no sense.

Some people believe a mothafucka won't kill somebody if he knows he's going to be executed. Who thinks of this shit? Ain't nobody thinking that far ahead, at least not where I come from. It's a rigged system based on lies, but that's not the worst part.

All of the arguments that support the death penalty assume everybody is guilty, but what if someone is innocent? The government has no answer if it makes a mistake. Even if they don't kill yo ass, if you've been on death row, you're fucked up. There's no way around it.

Everybody wants to talk about morality when it comes to killin' a mothafucka, but there ain't no moral conversation when it comes to somebody who ain't done shit. Where's the morality in that? How can there be support for a system that is based on bullshit that can make mistakes? But I'm not sure this government views killing innocent mothafuckas as a mistake. How the fuck do you find morality in some immoral shit? The government can target the poor and mothafuckas out of their mind, and if one or two happen to be innocent, that's just the cost of doing business in the name of justice.

This is some of the shit that I've thought about over the last 20 years since this 13-foot-long, 7-foot-wide, and 8-foot-high cell became my world. My innocence really doesn't matter at this point. If it did matter, it only mattered to me.

But the debt that I was given at birth has come due. Poverty practically places everyone in it on a form of death row. It's very hard to escape, and over time, it takes away your life, even if you still have a pulse.

When I started high school, I think we had 1000 students in our freshmen class, only 350 graduated. Of the 650 that did not graduate, the school district did not know what happened to 400 of them. I was one of the 400. My decision to stop attending school was as natural as breathing. Though I saw no reason for school, I loved to read. I loved how books took me to places that I had never heard of. It expanded my vocabulary. Whenever I came across a word I didn't understand, I would look it up in the dictionary. But I always felt I couldn't share my love of reading with anyone because they might think my ass was soft. You couldn't survive in my neighborhood if folks thought you were a bitch. Part of my reason for dropping out of school was to prove that I was no bitch.

No one from the school looked for me, and no one at home—if you can call it a home—ever asked: "Why aren't you in school?" Looking back, I think I was hoping somebody would notice that I wasn't in school.

Just as natural were the wrong choices I made for the lure of quick money. I settled for one of the few industries that would hire someone with no marketable skills except for watching for the cops and eventually beating up those that owed me money. But with that choice, I received the closest I would ever get to a diploma—a police record. The first step to death row, it read: "The individual that bears this criminal record can be considered for other crimes, especially when law enforcement is unable to locate a viable suspect."

I know you've heard it before—some inmate on death row protesting that he's innocent. Well, I'm not protesting anything. I already told my attorneys I don't want any last-minute appeals. I've seen how the courts work in this state. I've been on death row for 20 years and I've never seen or heard of a last-minute appeal saving anyone's ass. I've got about 12 hours to make peace with this bullshit, and I can't do that relying on some false hope to save my ass.

Right now, I'm on what you call suicide watch. In

other words, the government is watching my ass around the clock to make sure I don't kill myself so they can have the pleasure of doing it later this evening.

To call this place death row is accurate, but not for the reasons most think. You're faced with knowing you're going to die, but not knowing exactly when. But it's an environment that reminds us every day that we're going to die.

Most people have been on death row for at least 15 years. I heard Joe Morrison was on death row for almost 40 years before they got around to killing him. But that was before I got here.

Most of the people on death row shouldn't be here, not because they're innocent, some of them did some real nasty shit, but they have the IQ of a fucking walnut. That's one of America's dirty little secrets. Many of the inmates on death row don't know right from wrong, which makes them easy to kill. Death row is the slaughterhouse for humans.

And if you ain't crazy when you get to death row, chances are you will be by the time they kill yo ass. I'm in my cell for 23 hours a day, just me and my thoughts. I get one hour for exercise. How could you not be crazy? It's not natural to spend 23 hours in a space no bigger than a parking lot stall. Some of the older inmates also have physical shit to deal with—they had to wheel in Joe Morrison's ass to execute him because he could no longer walk. It's become common for prisoners to die on death row from an illness or natural causes before their execution date.

When Joe Morrison was finally executed, they did

him a favor. Each day, we get 86,400 seconds of life. Joe wasn't using his time, and if they freed him, he wouldn't know what to do with it. I wouldn't know what to do with my time if I were free. Being on death row has been the most stable, consistent, and predictable part of my life.

But death row is designed to take away hope. Hope is what separates humans from other animals. Animals don't have any knowledge of death. When you're on death row, you have too much knowledge of death, but you're like other animals because you have no sense of tomorrow.

Being on death row is like being at the zoo—a zoo that no one wants to visit. Those with all of their reasons for supporting the death penalty have no desire to stop by this shit. They don't want to see the animals in their cages. I don't want to see it.

When I was on trial, the first step was to take away my humanity. You can't have a death penalty if you're killing humans; you can only have it by killing "animals." This is the most important step because even if the "animal" is innocent, it is still an animal. Society accepts the possibility of killing innocent animals. No one thinks before eating a pork chop: "Was this pig innocent?" Doesn't matter… it was an animal and its purpose was to satisfy our hunger.

Death row operates in a similar way. "Was the person innocent?"

And society responds: "It doesn't matter; he was an animal. Besides, it satisfies the people's hunger for revenge."

BYRON WILLIAMS

As I sat in the courtroom, I remember some of the jurors looked at me with contempt. Unable to hide their feelings, their body language said: "Well, if he didn't do this, he's done something, so we better put an end to it right now." That's how a jury of my peers took less than 90 minutes to decide that I should die.

Soon, they will be asking what I want for my last meal. What I want I can't have. I long for my grandmother's oxtails, rice, collard greens, and hot water cornbread. And I want a loaf of bread to sop up the pot liquor. I can still taste those flavors in my mouth, along with the way my grandmother used to say, "Slow down when you eat, no need for it to come back up." The last time I saw her was at the trial when they sentenced me to die. She died of a stroke not long after that. Since I can't have her cooking, I guess I will have to settle for some Popeye's and sweet tea with a slice of sweet potato pie.

I have no idea what it will be like to knowingly experience my last meal. Will I slow down as my grandmother warned, or will I eat at my normal speed? I ate that way because I always had somewhere to go. I have somewhere to go tonight, but how fast I eat really ain't gonna matter. They gone make sure my ass is on time. I already feel like they trying to fatten me up for the slaughter that is to take place this evening.

The knowledge that death is near allows me to think about things I never considered before. How much of my life was wasted on shit that didn't matter but felt important in the moment? It is only as my life draws near its scheduled end that I realize the choices I made were not really my choices. That doesn't mean I'm not responsible for the choices, but poverty was influencing many of my decisions. If those Christians that come around here were really serious about predestination, they would be in the neighborhood where I grew up. But that predestation is not based on God's plan, but on poverty's.

Everything I did before being placed on death row was based on survival. Just as that jury was told to look at me as an animal, I looked at everyone around me with the same eyes. I had the ability to take a life because I thought, just like that district attorney, I would only be killing an animal. I woke up each day with survival on my mind. Anyone or anything that challenged my survival was a threat. My grandmother tried to convince me that was no way to live, but I wasn't about to listen to some old woman who was trying to teach me about being a man.

But my grandmother was the only family I really knew that felt like family. I knew my mother about the same way I knew Denzel Washington, from some photos and what other people said. I couldn't pick my father out of a lineup if he was the only man standing among a group of seated one-legged jockeys.

Red, from the movie Shawshank Redemption, was right—you only have two choices in prison: "Get busy living or get busy dying." Death row takes that first choice away. From the moment I heard the echoing finality of the prison doors close for the first time, even though I didn't realize it, I had begun the process of dying. It was appropriate that *The Count of Monte Cristo* was the last book I read. I don't want to be Edmund Dantès. I thought I did, but that was long before I read the book. Not now.

The shit that happened to Dantès was fucked up. It was the same shit that happened to me. I'm here because of an eyewitness testimony that never saw me, a district attorney that despised me, and a jury that wrongfully convicted me.

But unlike Dantès, this prison cell that has been my home for the last 15 years is better protected than the Château d'If. There's no escaping. And no one left my ass a massive treasure so that I could plot my revenge. But I had two things in common with Edmund Dantès. I'm in prison for something I didn't do but also had my own form of an abbé, a priest, to counsel me.

His name was George, that's all he told me. I knew he was a chaplain only by the fact he was allowed to enter death row. Even his demeanor was different from the other death row chaplains. He didn't wear one of those clerical collars, carried a Bible, or had a title, at least not one he shared with me. He would stop by to talk. It's funny how death row can also make you appreciate small shit like someone coming by to talk. I slowly appreciated that George was truly different; he never tried to make sense of my situation. He never gave me simple answers or asked the nature of my crime. Come to think of it, he didn't have to—he knew I wasn't here for stealing some French fries at Burger King.

George never condemned faith traditions that were not Christian. In fact, he welcomed them and said they made him a better Christian. I was shocked when he told me he didn't take the Bible literally but he took it seriously. At first, that shit didn't make sense to me. I guess I was used to those Bible belt mothafuckas that had all the goddamn answers.

When I asked George what was the difference between taking the Bible literally and seriously, he said, "I'm not interested in proving whether Moses parted the Red Sea or the three Hebrews survived the conditions of the fiery furnace, but the real value of these stories rested in what they mean for us today. Each of us has Red Sea experiences; we all have been unjustly hurled into the fiery furnace. These stories are metaphors of hope for our lives."

George's answer made sense to me. I trusted him. That's when I told him I was innocent. He seemed to believe me but didn't seem surprised.

After pausing, he shared with me that faith is not based on what he called "rewards and punishment" (good people are rewarded and bad people are punished). I laughed when he said that makes God sound too much like Santa Claus. George also told me the outcome of my life had no bearing on God's love for me.

Long before it was clear that I was to be executed, George asked me to consider how I might find peace, given my situation. He asked if I had the courage to trust God enough to pray for those responsible for my being on death row.

George didn't realize it, or maybe he did, but he was asking me to give up the one thing I had been holding onto. Not only would I have to give up any desire for revenge against Mrs. Morgenthau and the others, but I had to truly ask for them to be forgiven if I wanted to leave death row a free man.

I didn't immediately accept it—I wanted to cling to the comfort that revenge provided. But it wasn't revenge that was comforting. It was my anger. From death row, revenge would be difficult, but I could cling to my anger. Anger allowed me to always be the victim. With anger, my story began 20 years ago on death row, as if the first 25 years never happened. But as George and I continued to talk, the act of praying for my enemies had become more liberating. George told me that my pending execution wasn't my death sentence—anger was my executioner.

I came to realize there are lots of ways to die on death row before they kill you. Death row kills your humanity and your mind. But I had the power to make it well with my soul. And the only way I could do that was to pray for those who have prayed for this day for 20 years.

According to the scriptures, Jesus forgave his enemies as he hung on the cross. That shit never made any sense to me until this moment. I must pray for my enemies because it is the only way I can die a free man. George taught me that forgiveness is the most selfish act of our faith journey because it's not about the person that has harmed us but it is the deal God made with me to find peace.

My selfish ass must pray for Mrs. Morgenthau, who believed she was doing the right thing when she testified against me. I must pray for the district attorney who did everything possible to prove I wasn't human to make it as easy as possible to put me on death row. And I must also pray for the jury, armed with only circumstantial evidence but found me guilty beyond a reasonable doubt.

"Father, forgive them for they don't know what they have done. I ask not for vengeance, but peace for all. I pray that you might use them so they may touch others in order to prevent what will happen to me this evening. Amen."

I hear the guards coming. They are bringing my last supper. George will be here soon to take the final walk with me. We've already agreed we will exchange no words once he gets here—no scripture, no last-minute prayers. Nothing else needs to be said, except to ask George to contact *Books on the Inside* so they can stop sending books.

I'm ready, my Lord.

CHAPTER 6

Profile in Courage

Jake Parker was a rising political star in his party. The young member of the House of Representatives was popular in his district and had received national media attention on the cable news outlets. The future looked bright for the young congressman, until he was forced to make a tough vote that could derail his promising career.

This is otherwise known as the "profile in courage moment." Taken for the title of Senator John F. Kennedy's 1957 Pulitzer Prize-winning text. It was an examination of the courage that a handful of members of Congress exhibited at crucial moments in history, disregarding the political consequences of their actions in order to do what he believed to be the right thing for the country. This is the decision that awaits young Parker.

AT 27, JAKE PARKER had won an improbable primary victory against House Representative David Kaufman, Chair of the powerful Rules Committee. Since the seat was safely in Parker's party, his victory in the upcoming November election was all but assured.

Parker was young, photogenic, and charismatic. He spoke in a manner that, regardless of the crowd size, conveyed to all in attendance he was speaking exclusively to them. Infusing his campaign with a feeling of youth and vigor, he would frequently remind those on the campaign trail, "The era of the old ways has come to an unmerciful end. It's time for a new wave of leadership." And Parker presented himself as the one riding that wave of change while portraying Kaufman as helplessly tethered to the inefficient past.

Winning the primary against Kaufman was consistent with everything else that had seemingly gone right in his life—it was predestined, at least that is what he believed. Parker ran on a series of issues that appealed to voters, illustrating how Kaufman was out of touch with his district—a victim of the cesspool that was Washington DC.

During the campaign, Parker developed a rapport with the voters by formulating simplified explanations for complex issues that he encased in certainty. He effectively won his race against Kaufman two weeks before the election. During a press conference, a reporter asked Kaufman how he planned to vote on H.R. 2120. H.R. was an infrastructure legislation that would extend an oil pipeline, which could potentially bring jobs to Kaufman's district. Though Kaufman was leaning toward supporting the legislation, he responded by saying:

"I don't know. I like most of the legislation, but I must do my due diligence before my vote because, as with all legislation, especially something of this size, the devil is always in the details."

With three words, Kaufman proved, Parker right; he was out of touch. Kaufman wrongly assumed his time in Washington had earned him the right to invoke nuance and his district would give him the benefit of the doubt. But instead, in three words, Kaufman wrote his political obituary: "I don't know." Parker's political team quickly seized on the opportunity, releasing a statement that he "WOULD" vote for H.R. 2120, which would bring much-needed jobs to the district. Mocking Kaufman, he said repeatedly, "'I don't know' was a euphemism for 'I don't care about the district'." He ran multiple political ads that all ended with "David Kaufman may not know, but the people of this district know; it's time for a change!" The voters agreed by giving Parker 54% of their vote.

Parker arrived in Washington on the heels of his perfunctory November victory. With his party in the majority, he seemed poised to carry out the agenda he promised the people of his district. H.R. 2120 failed to make it out of committee during the last session of Congress, but a revised version was ready for discussion. Parker publicly stated his intention to vote for the legislation, reassuring his constituents via newsletters and online webinars of his intention. With his party's majority in the House, the bill, this time, easily made it out of committee.

With the bill soon to make it to the floor of the House of Representatives, Parker sat in his office as his chief staff, Maxwell Perdy, entered, "Congressman Parker, we need to talk, sir."

"What is it, Max? You looked troubled!"

"I am," Perdy said.

"Let's have it. It seems I only hear about things when it's bad news."

"I think you need to meet with young Reynolds who we hired out of Georgetown... he's done some analysis on the infrastructure bill."

"Sounds like I'm not going to like what young Reynolds has to say."

"You won't, sir, but you have to hear it."

Parker called his executive assistant, "Ivy, find Reynolds and tell him to come to my office."

Ten minutes later, there was a knock on the door. Perdy opened the door, and standing there was someone who appeared much younger than his 25 years would indicate. Reynolds stood 6-foot-tall, weighing 150 lbs., but only if a 10-pound dumbbell were attached. He was wearing a rumpled brown suit that seemed to be the only item in his work wardrobe rotation. His brown penny loafers appeared to be in dire need of shine. But his wire-frame glasses with cable temples conveyed expertise in the subject matter. At least that's how Parker perceived him after slowly looking Reynolds over, starting with his feet.

"Come in, Reynolds," Perdy said. "I was just informing Congressman Parker that you needed to speak with him about the infrastructure legislation."

Appearing somewhat uncomfortable, Reynolds responded, "Yes, that's correct."

"Well, what is it?" Parker said sternly.

"After going over the numbers multiple times and

comparing my findings with the Congressional Budget Office, I am of the conclusion that if this bill passes, it will cost your district roughly 5,000 jobs. The CBO will make their findings public tomorrow."

Undeterred, Parker responded, "But I've seen estimates that suggest this legislation will bring 7,500 jobs to the area, so it's a net plus of 2,500 jobs."

"Well, sir, that's the other problem. It looks like this project will at best bring 1,000 jobs to the area. So, if this legislation passes, it could cost roughly 4,000 jobs."

"What?" Parker screamed. "How can that be? I had assurances from the lobbyist that this project was a job creator. My support for this legislation is why they backed my campaign."

"That's an old lobbyist ploy, especially when someone is running for the first time and they believe he can win. Remember, they wrote the legislation that went into committee. They give you the best-case scenario that you wanted to hear, and in exchange, they and their friends gave you nice size campaign contributions. And they're depending on you not finding out until several years after the ground is broken and the project is underway."

Turning toward his junior colleague, Perdy added, "But fortunately, we have Reynolds here to catch it before it is too late."

With a look of consternation, Parker shot back, "I don't see what's fortunate about it!"

"It's fortunate because now you can vote against the legislation, especially with the CBO analysis coming out tomorrow."

"I can't do that!"

"Sir, you have to! It's a job killer in your district."

As the conversation became more intense, Parker looked over Perdy's shoulder and calmly said to Reynolds, "That will be all for now, Reynolds. Thank you."

"Thank you, sir!"

With Reynolds gone, Parker immediately turned toward Perdy, visibly upset, "Allow me to remind you, though it should be painstakingly clear, this the office of Congressman Jake Ryan Parker! Therefore, everyone in this office serves at my pleasure and I will not tolerate insubordination from my chief of staff, especially in front of junior staff. Do I make myself clear?"

"Yes, Congressman Parker," Perdy replied.

"You were Congressman Kaufman's Chief of Staff, and I retained you at the behest of the Speaker. I hope I haven't misjudged your loyalty?"

"No, sir! Actually, it is because of my loyalty to this office that I spoke, albeit out of turn. It's your interests that I'm thinking of," Perdy said.

"Frankly, I don't think this is a problem. The people sent me here, in part, to represent their interest, which includes voting for this infrastructure bill," Parker said.

"But you have information they do not have. The people you represent have jobs and lives and don't have the time to pay attention to what goes on in Washington. That's why they sent you to represent them."

"How's it going to look when, on the first piece of major legislation, I vote against the interests of my constituents?"

"Sir, you have Reynolds and they don't."

"Come on, Perdy! I can't trot out a 25-year-old snot-nose kid fresh out of Georgetown and say, 'I know you wanted me to vote for this legislation that will bring jobs to the district, but this young man says that's wrong. So, I've got to go with him.' Reynolds reeks of everything they hate about Washington and coastal elites. How do you think that's going to play back home?"

"It's going to look like, in your first term, you already experienced your Profiles in Courage moment."

"My what?"

"Your Profiles in Courage moment. *Profiles in Courage* was a book written by President Kennedy, while he was in the Senate. It is a series of short biographies that described acts of courage by members of the United States Senate. The book won the Pulitzer Prize."

"Sounds to me like you're saying I should risk my seat in the House and it's not even warm yet."

"Not at all, sir. I don't see how you can vote for legislation that you know is going to cost jobs in your district."

"You mean what somebody believes will cost jobs? They don't really know."

"There's no exact science, but we do know those that are behind this infrastructure bill will benefit financially. We know they backed your campaign, and it's unclear if your district will prosper as they believe. That's hardly a formula you can take back to the voters."

"But can I vote against it and get reelected?"

"That depends on who is driving—you or your ambition? If it's you, then you will do what you need to do so you can sleep at night. If, however, it's your ambition... well, I think that answers itself in terms of your vote."

"You don't think I should vote for it!"

"Right now, you've taken a position based on what several people have said. That position is being challenged by several other people. As it stands right now, sir, I think you should do your due diligence, find out as much about the legislation as possible. Where is it weak? Where is it strong? If there are things that need to be fixed, offer amendments and then see."

"I'm not sure I can do it."

"It's your responsibility to pick the best out of several bad choices. There will be a lot of pressure on you, should it get out that you're wavering, but I believe in what you stand for, that's why I wanted to remain as your chief of staff after you defeated Kaufman. If you're having some reservations about the legislation, the first thing you need to do is notify Melvin Barnes. As your biggest backer and champion of this infrastructure legislation, you need to share with him your misgivings."

"Thank you, Perdy, your council and loyalty means a lot. I guess I better get Barnes on the phone."

Barnes was one of the leading political operatives in Washington DC, his firm behind the infrastructure legislation. His group had given campaign contributions to more than half of the members in the House Representatives and Senate, regardless of party. Barnes liked to say at his organization's closed-door annual meetings: "Folks there is a man who has the current president's cell phone number, and when he calls, the president answers. Six years ago, that same man had the last president's cell phone number and that president also answered when he called, even though he was from the other party. And ladies and gentlemen, with your support, I expect to continue to be that man!"

When Barnes got wind that Kaufman was in political trouble back home, coupled with the fact that Kaufman was never keen on the infrastructure legislation even though he suggested during campaign he was leaning toward it, Barnes viewed him as an unreliable vote. Having not forgotten how Kaufman opposed the last version of the bill, Barnes seized the opportunity to ingratiate himself with Parker after polling suggested Kaufman was vulnerable. Barnes presented his fundraising prowess as a mechanism to support good government. And all he wanted in return was Parker's support for the infrastructure legislation that Kaufman was unable to see. Parker naively saw it as a benign request because the true beneficiaries would be the people of his district.

Barnes suggested that he and Parker meet for lunch at The Old Ebbitt Grill—the oldest restaurant in Washington. Barnes had the use of a private room; it was where he held all of his important business meetings, this is where he met Parker. Parker was surprised to see several men had accompanied Barnes to the lunch meeting, which he assumed was to be a one-on-one affair. He recognized the gentlemen as individuals, originally introduced by Barnes that contributed to his campaign.

At 6'4" and 270 lbs., externally, Barnes possessed a fun-loving personality that matched his physical stature. But right behind his eyes was the ruthlessness of a rattlesnake and Barnes was shrewd enough to allow individuals to catch a glimpse of what lies beneath, his way of warning potential adversaries to back off. When Parker entered the private room and Barnes rose to greet him warmly, the young congressman could sense the preemptive warning nestled in the glint within the big man's eyes.

"It's so nice to see you again, Congressman Parker. I was thrilled to get your invitation for lunch. Now, before we get down to any business, Naomi, could you come here a minute, darling?"

A stunningly attractive woman with brunette hair, who was standing just outside the door, appeared wearing a svelte black Alexander McQueen single-breasted suit and matching Ferragamo pump shoes with the vara bow.

"Yes, Mr. Barnes," she said.

"Honey, will you bring the Congress a shot of Macallan 25? Make it neat. And be sure to tell Robinson to put a drop of water in it to open it up."

"Will do, Mr. Barnes."

Parker remained fixated on the door for several seconds after Naomi exited until Barnes' booming voice caught his attention. Putting his arm around Parker, he said:

"Let me tell you a story. There was a little puppy that was crossing the railroad tracks and he didn't see the train coming and it took off part of his tail. The puppy, so distraught, went back to pick up his tail and another train from the opposite direction took off his head. Now do you know what the moral of that story is?" Barnes asked.

"No, I don't," Parker said, looking somewhat bewildered.

"Never lose your head for a little piece of tail!"

And with one of Barnes' famous backslaps, the room exploded in raucous laughter.

"Goddamn, Melvin, you've been telling that story for 30 years and it's still funny!" one of the meeting attendees said.

Barnes' story put Parker at ease. He sat down, dined on grilled mussels, listened to more of Barnes' tall tales, enjoying a second Macallan after lunch. He was unaware that Barnes had silenced the room by way of eye contact.

"Congressman," Barnes said with a smile. "I've been in this business a long time, I've seen a lot of people, good people, come and go. One thing my daddy told me a long time ago still holds true, he said, 'Son, when someone begins a conversation with 'But I thought…' there is usually a problem lurking close behind.' Now, when I got your phone call wanting to meet with me, I got the sneaking, uncomfortable feeling that you were saying: 'This was a but I thought conversation.' Please tell me I'm wrong."

Parker, almost choking on the Macallan, didn't know what to say. Barnes' charming smile was a distant memory and everyone in the room was staring at him. The silence was deafening.

"Well, since you brought it up," Parker said.

"I didn't bring up shit. You brought it up when you called me because you're chicken shit ass suddenly has cold feet on the infrastructure bill!" Barnes snapped.

Parker was stunned. *How does Barnes know? Someone must have leaked the information. It was probably Perdy*, he thought.

"Oh, hell boy, don't look so surprised, you think this is my first rodeo?" Barnes asked. There's only two things you and I have in common—money for your campaign, and you got a shitload of that, and my infrastructure bill that you promised to support."

"But some say that bill is going to cost my district jobs," Parker said.

"Who put a fool idea in your head like that? You probably been reading that bullshit that the CBO puts out. Don't you know if they ain't against something, they got no reason to be in business. I been fighting with them all my political life, and I'm still standing."

"I can't support the bill if it will cost my district jobs," Parker said.

"It won't cost your district jobs."

"But what if it does?" Parker asked.

Now the full force of Barnes' ire came forth. "I JUST TOLD YOU IT WON'T! You think this is some kinda 'Mr. Goes to Washington' bullshit? You take my money, drink my liquor, eat my food, stare at my women, you gave me your word, and now because some number crunchers in your office tells you there might be a problem, you want to turn your back on those who are responsible for your being here?

Turning his back to Parker, Barnes looked sternly at one of his associates and said, "Fred, I think we got us a one-term Congressman that nobody will remember in two years."

A voice from the other side of the room cried out, "Melvin, Parker is new. No need to be so heavy-handed with the young man. Let's work with him so he can see how this bill will benefit his district."

"You're right, Bill," Barnes said. Turning back to Parker, "Congressman, I'm sorry for speaking to you that way. I've worked so hard on this legislation, only to have a key vote walk in to say they might have second thoughts... it threw me. But I have no cause to speak to a member of the House of Representatives in that manner. My apologies, sir."

Parker, visibly shaken, agreed to work with Barnes' team to improve the legislation. Parker saw it as a tepid victory. For the first time, his eyes were truly opened. He still believed he was sent to Washington to represent the people who put him there. Parker realized it wasn't the tens of thousands of voters; it was the interests of Barnes and his powerful cabal that he represented. His district overwhelmingly supported the infrastructure legislation that he was now convinced, based on his treatment, was not in their long-term economic interests because that's what Barnes told them to think through his effective propaganda campaign. Parker saw himself as no different than the sycophants that sat around the table at lunch laughing on cue at the same jokes Barnes had been telling for decades.

By the time Parker returned to his Capitol Hill

office, phones were ringing nonstop, emails flooded his office, his cell phones, personal and House-issued, suddenly blew up with calls and texts. It seemed word had leaked back in his district that he might be wavering on the infrastructure bill.

In the midst of what suddenly became a chaotic atmosphere, Ivy notified Parker that the Speaker of the House wanted to see him immediately. *There could only be one reason the Speaker would want to meet with a first-term member of Congress*, Parker thought. Realizing Barnes had no intention of working with him on the legislation, Parker felt duped again. And now he had to face the muscle of the Speaker.

The Speaker's office was organically intimidating—it oozed with power. Within its walls were the secrets of how legislative deals had been created since the Constitution was ratified in 1788. Within the confines of the office, Herman Rutledge, the current Speaker, who stood 5' 8," appeared larger than Melvin Barnes.

Parker was wary of the Speaker's warm greeting, having received Barnes' treatment several hours earlier.

"Well, freshman, it seems like you got yourself in quite a twist," Rutledge said.

"Apparently, someone leaked a statement that wasn't accurate," Parker responded.

"Son, the last time there was a leak this size, Noah built himself a boat!" Rutledge said.

"Melvin Barnes is behind this," Parker lamented.

"Probably so, but that's not why I wanted to see you." Rearing back in his plush leather Speaker's chair, Rutledge said, "There are two types of people in the

House of Representatives—policy people and numbers people. I'm a numbers person. And my numbers tell me you may not be with us anymore, is that true?

"Mr. Speaker, I have some concerns."

"Hell, Parker, everybody's got concerns. That's called making legislation."

"Why is my vote so important? Why is there suddenly pressure on me?" Parker asked.

"Because you're in a safe seat! If I lose your vote, after you've already gone public with your intentions to support the legislation, then those in competitive districts, already primed to jump like a flea off a dog's ass, will change their vote and the legislation is dead."

"Couldn't we delay it and come back with a better bill?"

"This is the delay and this is the better bill, we won't get another bite out of this apple. We pass this bill in the House, we already got the votes in the Senate, we could be in the majority for another decade at least."

"My gut tells me this bill is wrong."

"And my gut tells me I may be looking at a one-term Congressman."

That was the second time it was presented to Parker that this vote might cost him his seat. And it was done so by men with power beyond idle threat-making.

Rutledge added, "The first time you sat in my office, I quoted the great former Speaker, Sam Rayburn, 'The best way to get along is to go along!' The rules for voting in the majority are simple—vote your district and vote your conscience. But when your speaker needs your vote, you vote with your speaker. Welcome to Congress,

I need your vote on this one and I don't need any surprises. It's just that simple."

"Mr. Speaker, I don't know."

Parker paused. He recalled how those three words were so crucial to his victory against Kaufman. He remembered mocking Kaufman when he said, "'I don't know' was a euphemism for 'I don't care about the district'." Now he was saying those words honestly and openly. But Parker, unlike Kaufman, said those words in front of the Speaker and not a press conference. But Rutledge was unsympathetic to the first-year congressman.

"That's why I'm the Speaker!" Rutledge snapped. "Because I do know! I wish folks would bring me legislation that was perfect. I also wish I had the number to Jennifer Aniston's cell phone and she took my calls, but that ain't how it works! I'm not saying this bill is going to cost jobs in your district because I don't believe it will. If I did think that, I would join you in opposing it."

"But Reynolds is confident this legislation will cost jobs," Parker responded meekly.

"Who the fuck is Reynolds?" Rutledge snapped. "Some goddamn boy wonder, I presume. Do you know how many of them have paced these halls never to be heard from again since I've been in Congress? Does Reynolds have a vote on the House floor?"

"I can go back to the district and tell the people the truth about this legislation," Parker said.

"Do you know what the truth is?"

"I know what the CBO says. I know what my

legislative aide says."

"Both may be right, but let me tell you what several decades on Capitol Hill has taught me... people don't give a shit about what's true, they care about what they believe. And they believe this bill will bring jobs. Moreover, ignorance binds people together much tighter than truth—it always has and it always will."

"Either way, I've got to go back to the district and tell them what I'm feeling."

"I think that's a good idea. You've got a decision to make that's harder than a lignum knot. But I don't know of too many people in their first year on Capitol Hill that made an enemy out of Melvin Barnes and lasted," Rutledge said.

Parker decided to return to his district to face the voters. He felt he owed it to them. He asked Perdy to accompany him. On the flight to his district, Parker lamented to Perdy, "I've never encountered anyone as powerful as Barnes. I've heard about people like him, but I didn't think they really existed. Even my hometown newspaper will be out to get me if I don't vote for the legislation."

"There's no doubting Barnes is a formidable enemy," Perdy said.

"Formidable? He creates allies out of people that don't even know he exists! He wields power from within the shadows! I feel like I'm fighting water."

"Congressman, do you know how you're going to vote?"

"I don't know," Parker said.

Once again, Parker was arrested by those three

words that once represented the pathway to a seat in the House of Representatives, but now they were a source of contrition. Parker recognized "I don't know" was not a form weakness that he ignorantly labeled Kaufman, but a sign of strength—the type of integrity that was required to be a member of the House of Representatives. In hearing himself repeat the words he derided Kaufman for uttering, he felt shame. If he could pick up the phone, or better still, issue a public apology, he would.

Parker turned to Perdy, "I'm going to oppose the legislation. I'm going to explain to the people that I'm not opposed to the legislation but that I'm opposed to the bait and switch used to financially benefit a few on the front end while leaving the hardworking people in my district holding the bag."

"If that's what you're going to say, we better start crafting the speech."

"No, I will write this speech myself. My words only," Parker said.

"I understand, Congressman," Perdy replied somewhat surprised by his boss's newfound political courage. "Will you excuse me, sir? I need to send directives to the district office as to how we're going to handle the response from your speech."

"By all means," Parker said.

When Parker and his team arrived at the event, they had not anticipated the spectacle. It was a packed auditorium with an additional several hundred outside that were unable to get in, all primed to a feverish pitch in anticipation of his remarks. They held placards that read: "Jobs Not Jowls." They repeated the chant ad nauseam as Parker made his way to the podium.

Parker raised his hands, urging for calm. The silence became deafening until a voice broke through, "You better not let us down, you son-of-a-bitch!" The crowd once again returned to the chant, "Jobs Not Jowls."

Parker finally got the crowd subdued. Everyone was seated with the exception of Barnes and the major contributors to Parker's campaign. They stood against the back wall directly in Parker's line of vision.

"My friends," Parker opened. "It seems there have been a lot of leaks about how I was going to vote on the infrastructure bill that will soon make its way to the House floor. As Speaker Rutledge said to me the other day, 'The last time there was a leak of this size, Noah built himself a boat.'" Parker's remarks were greeted with polite laughter, but as he read the body language in the room, it was clear there was only one thing they came to hear, and jokes wouldn't lessen the disappointment.

"I came here today because I didn't want the people of this district, that I am proud to represent, to hear how I planned to vote through any source other than my own words looking you straight in the eye."

Holding his speech above his head, Parker said, "I have here the speech that I was prepared to give."

Throwing the speech behind him, Parker then said, "Hell, you don't need a speech, you just need to know that I AM VOTING FOR THE INFRASTRUCTURE BILL!"

Joyous pandemonium erupted as Barnes and his

team quietly exited the building. Inexplicably, people were now holding placards that read: "Thank you, Congressman Parker, for keeping your word!"

Through the cheers, Perdy asked, "I thought you were going to vote against the bill? What happened?"

Parker, grinning, said, "It was two things. First, you said this might be my "Profiles in Courage" moment. I picked up a copy of that book. Not one of those people that Kennedy talked about had courage in their first term, which reminded me of something my pastor used to say: 'Get you some authority before you try to use it.' Second thing, Barnes notified me. He promised not only to put his full weight behind my future reelections, but he also promised to help with a special campaign if this bill doesn't deliver."

"That was it?" Perdy asked.

"There was one more thing. Running for office is a lot like going for a long drive and deciding who is going to drive—your conscience or your ambition. I decided to let my ambition take the wheel, at least through my second term."

The next day, back in Washington, Perdy walked into The Old Ebbitt Grill and the maître d recognized him immediately, "Welcome, Mr. Perdy! Mr. Barnes and his group are expecting you in the private room."

"Thank you, Carl."

When Perdy entered the room, a thunderous applause went up. Barnes walked over and put his large arms around him. He told the excited crowd, "Perdy, my boy, you were magnificent. And tell the Speaker that I'm indebted to him for suggesting that you remained as

Parker's chief of staff. It was masterful."

In Parker's district, a local newspaper ran an editorial praising his courage. It was entitled: "Freshman congressman shows old pols how to get things done in Washington!"

CHAPTER 7

The President's Inferno

Inferno, written by Dante Aligheiri in the 14th century, commonly referred to as Dante's Inferno, is the inspiration for this story. Just as Inferno describes Dante's journey through Hell, Justice does similar, guiding the last 43 men who served as president through the final rings of Hell. This serves as the amoral critique on the American presidency.

ON THE EVENING of January 6, 2021, the 43 men that had served as America's president had a rendezvous with their own inferno. Each lamented the day's activities that saw, for the first time, America's 233-year history of peaceful transfer of power be brought to a violent end. Not since the Civil War had the fragility of America's democratic-republican form of government been so tested.

The beasts of arrogance, hubris, and pride, chased the presidents through a dark forest. The straightforward pathway had been lost—they ended up at what seemed to be an abandoned cave, secured by a gate. They saw a human figure standing near the gate, but it was unclear if it was a man or merely a shadow.

With nowhere to turn and the beasts seemingly gaining, they put aside some of their fears and turned to the mysterious man for help.

"Can you help us?" Mr. Jefferson said, somewhat panicked.

"Certainly," the man said calmly. "I've been expecting you."

"How, sir, is it possible that you've been expecting us when I don't know how we ended up here?" Mr. Madison said.

"It is not an accident that you ended up here tonight."

"What does that mean, sir?" Mr. Lincoln asked.

"It means that each of you, in your own unique way, are among the pillars of American democracy. Mr. Jefferson, you condensed two centuries of Enlightenment thinking into a single canonized sentence that serves as the frame protecting the canvas of the Constitution that Mr. Madison wrote. It was Mr. Lincoln's belief in those documents, especially the Declaration of Independence that held the Union together. And 67 years after Mr. Lincoln's presidency, Mr. Roosevelt came along to remind a nervous nation in the throes of the Depression, "The only thing we have to fear is fear itself."

"Excuse me," Mr. Madison interrupted. "I've always wanted to ask Mr. Roosevelt, what does the 'only thing we have to fear is fear itself' actually mean? It sounds to me like inspired nonsense."

"Well," Mr. Roosevelt responded, ever smiling. "I

wouldn't expect you to fully understand. I suspect the only reason you are here is because of your work on the Constitution. It certainly would not be for anything memorable you did as president, which bears a corresponding relationship with your diminutive size."

Ever mindful that at 5'4", he was the nation's shortest, Madison shot back, "I demand satisfaction, sir!"

"Mr. Madison," Roosevelt said. "The only satisfaction that you shall receive from me is my indebtedness to you for crafting our first Constitution, a document, though not a perfect instrument, provided a firm base upon which all manner of humans, of all races and colors and creeds, could build our solid structure of democracy. Beyond that, your legacy is one dominated by the contours of Mr. Jefferson's shadow."

"Quite a statement from a man who cannot walk. Did you forget your dependence on the rest of us to get you to the gate where we now stand, lest you would have been devoured by those ravishing beasts that were chasing us?"

"Gentlemen! Gentlemen!" that mysterious man shot back. "You were not brought here to bicker among yourselves, but to look at the present moment and determine the shadow that it might cast, if any, on your legacy."

"Do you have a name, sir?" Mr. Madison asked.

"You can refer to me as "Justice."

"You know first the servant that took care of me was named 'Jupiter'," Mr. Jefferson said. "I wonder if there are any relations? Have you spent any time in Albemarle County?"

"Oh, I've been everywhere, Mr. Jefferson," Justice responded.

Justice led the presidents through the gates of hell, which Justice said was necessary if the presidents were to avoid the three beasts that he encountered earlier. A haunting inscription marked the gates: "Abandon all hope, you who enter here!"

Frightened and uncertain of their direction, the presidents ventured deeper into the darkness of the unknown. Justice told the presidents that he was sent by America's rich democratic commitments to liberty and equality to reassure them their actions had no bearing on the tragic events that unfolded earlier on Capitol Hill.

Suddenly, a scene at the Constitutional Convention in 1787 illuminated the darkness. It was followed by President James Monroe signing a document in 1820, followed by President Millard Fillmore performing a similar task in 1850.

"I recognize the first scene," Mr. Madison blurted. "I was there."

"I recognize the second scene," Mr. Monroe exclaimed.

"And I certainly recognize the third scene," Mr. Fillmore said.

"Glad to see that you remember, especially you, Mr. Fillmore, for I fear, given your brief and rather unremarkable presidency, this may be the only highlight of your presidency, and thus may be the final time we hear from you on our journey," Justice said.

"But what does it mean and why have you brought us here?" President Franklin Pierce asked.

"Welcome to the first ring of hell. It is defined by limbo," Justice said.

The presidents were witnessing the signing of the Constitution, the Missouri Compromise, and the Compromise of 1850 respectively.

"Gentlemen," Justice said. "In each case, the compromise enacted were an attempt to find a middle ground of the issue of slavery."

"Compromise is the essential element of our form of government," Mr. Monroe said.

"Perhaps," Justice said calmly. "But each scene offers a dysfunctional through line that reveals American dependency on racial capitalism. And America would continue this practice for the foreseeable future."

"You're missing the point," Mr. Madison exclaimed. "Compromise is an integral aspect of America's democratic-republican form of government."

"I would agree in the abstract, but would anyone argue that the aforementioned "compromises" produced a net positive for American democracy?" Justice said.

"But without the Three-Fifths Compromise that counted male slaves as three-fifths for census purposes, there would not have been a United States as we know it today, and all the colonies would have been vulnerable to foreign invasion," Mr. Madison said defensively.

"Mr. Madison, you, along with the other members of the convention, assaulted the English language in order to avoid using the word "slave" in the

Constitution. If there was nothing wrong with owning other human beings, why not say it expressly?" Justice said.

"We had to do it, lest we would not have had a complete country. The North and the South would have been too divided to unite. And slavery was the divisive issue," Mr. Madison said.

"Couldn't Misters Monroe and Fillmore make the same argument about the compromises they signed as well as others not mentioned? The Missouri Compromise of 1820 was passed to preserve the balance of power in Congress between slave and free states. What you fail to consider is that the Declaration of Independence, written by Mr. Jefferson and the others on the committee, was a moral document—a signed commitment to the virtues of liberty and equality," Justice said.

"Sir, what's your point?" President John Tyler asked.

"Interesting coming from you, Mr. Tyler, given that 16 years after your presidency, you joined the Confederate government—the only former president to do so. America was founded on liberty and equality, but when it came to the descendants from Africa, you looked for compromises to justify the unjustifiable. America sought compromise as a pathway to appropriate Native American lands in order to spur Westward Expansion. You can't have a country based on liberty and equality and seek to get by on compromises when it comes to owning people stealing land. To be generous, it places one in moral limbo,"

Justice said.

"Sir, I fear your naivety about politics causes you to oversimplify matters," Tyler said.

"America had a number of compromises that achieved three things, while failing the most important. Though the compromises cited may have benefitted perceived immediate gratifications, they were one-sided deals that advanced the notions of racial capitalism and empire, while managing to kick the slavery question down the road until 1861," Justice said.

"Why was this such a failure?" Mr. Tyler asked.

"There can be no compromise when the issue is human dignity," Justice said firmly.

Then Justice took the presidents through another door, where two men from the early 19th century, dressed in buckskin, were walking toward a Native American settlement.

Mr. Jefferson quickly spoke up. "This is a scene from the Corps of Discovery Expedition I commissioned."

"What?" President Andrew Jackson asked.

"Mr. Jackson, you probably refer to it as the Louis and Clark Expedition," Mr. Jefferson responded dismissively.

"Right again, Mr. Jefferson. This is the Louis and Clark Expedition, but it is also America's official foray into greed," Justice said.

"You obviously do not understand politics, sir!"

"Gentlemen, it's pointless to respond defensively by pointing to my political ignorance. I may not fully understand politics, but I understand avarice. I understand how easy it is for an amoral paradigm like politics to create its version of morality in order to proceed with its objectives."

"How else were we to realize what the newly acquired territory bore without an expedition?" Jefferson asked.

"That's an interesting phrase 'newly acquired territory.' I assume you're referring to the Louisiana Purchase and the land you bought from Napoleon?" Liberty said.

"Of course, sir. That deal doubled the size of the nation."

"Mr. Jefferson, you gave this fledgling nation imperishable language, declaring that liberty and equality were to be the touchstones of the American experiment. You proceeded to write in the *Declaration* a list of indictments against Great Britain. Though you ultimately won your battle to formally secede as a British colony, you conveniently decided to maintain the ideals of empire inherited from your British brethren for your own economic benefit."

"I assume, sir, you are referring to my book, Notes on the State of Virginia, that I advanced as a suspicion only, that the blacks—whether originally a distinct race or made distinct by time and circumstances—are inferior to the whites in the endowments both of body and mind," Jefferson said.

"That's part of it, but there's also those that you referred to in the *Declaration* as 'merciless savages.' How is it you can suggest the Louisiana Purchase was 'newly acquired territory' already inhabited by others?"

"Sovereignty requires that the United States

establish and maintain its sphere of influence," Mr. Jefferson said.

"That sounds like a doctrine dependent on the belief that the white skin is superior," Justice said.

"I believe my thoughts on the subject are documented in my book, sir," Mr. Jefferson said.

Justice shot back, "But shortly after the Louisiana Purchase, Thomas Paine and Joel Barlow met with you to discuss an opportunity for a restart, to move the nation closer to the ideals of liberty and equality contained in the Declaration. They appealed to you to prohibit slavery in Louisiana, use German immigrants and freed slaves, proposing that you offer land grants as an enticement. You declined largely because of the Haitian Revolution. You feared that a similar uprising might make its way to America."

"We were a fledgling nation, sir. The Louisiana Purchase was a massive undertaking. I couldn't consider the issue of emancipation on any level along with the need to expand the country," Mr. Jefferson said.

"You meant the empire, right?" Justice asked.

"If you are attempting to conflate the United States' declaration of liberty with the colonial despotism of Great Britain, I must protest, sir!" Mr. Jefferson said.

With slow and measured claps of the hand, Justice responded sarcastically, "Well said, Mr. Jefferson! For a man known more for the rhapsodic inspiration of his written words than his impassioned speech, your last statement was uncharacteristically impressive. Could it be, your words were meant not for me specifically but for the other 42 men in attendance, who, by virtue of being president, have also taken a silent oath to uphold some measure of American hypocrisy?"

"What hypocrisy do you speak of, sir?" Mr. Jefferson asked.

"The preservation of hypocrisy may very well be the one characteristic that binds you together," Justice said.

"Mr. Jefferson, I'm afraid this fella is correct, we are galvanized by hypocrisy. And to be president is to accept some inconsistency between what we said and what we do," Mr. Lincoln said.

"I certainly don't see it as hypocritical," Mr. Jefferson said.

"You don't, Mr. Jefferson?" Justice asked. "You wrote everyone is equal, but you owned people."

Then Justice, staring at Mr. Madison, said, "You wrote a Constitution that gave the institution of slavery constitutional legitimacy. Though the preamble of the Constitution begins: 'We the People,' the original intended beneficiaries were delineated by race, gender, and class. Doesn't that sound hypocritical?"

Justice added, "There is not one of you, from President Washington to the present, that did not oversee, at least with the silence of consent, the preservation of racial capitalism. It is the ugly secret that fortifies America's economic engine."

"I think you oversimplify matters," Mr. Nixon said. "Being president sometimes means finding the best solution within a series of bad choices."

"Perhaps!" Justice said. "But it doesn't mitigate that, in addition to being commander in chief of the armed forces, you also oversee hypocrisy. That includes you, Mr. Obama."

A hush went over those in attendance as all eyes were fixed on Mr. Obama and how he might respond. John Kennedy's Catholicism represented the only diversity for a lot that was white, male, and protestant... until Mr. Obama.

"I am not accusing any of you of intentional maleficence. Mr. Obama's Justice Department gets high marks for the way it quietly reshaped the so-called 'war on drugs,' but part of the hypocrisy rests with his indiscriminate use of drone strikes," Justice said.

"The truth is," Mr. Obama said. "The technology really began to take off right at the beginning of my presidency. And it wasn't until about a year to a year and a half in where I began to realize that the Pentagon and our national-security apparatus and the CIA were all getting too comfortable with the technology as a tool to fight terrorism."

"Fair enough, but was there a significant escalation in drone strikes during your second year? Wasn't 2010 a bloodier year for drone strikes in the Middle East region than 2009?"

Justice continued, "Even though you made great strides in curbing the insanity created by the ongoing war on drugs, you still arrested more people during your time as president for marijuana-related offenses than Wall Street greed."

"I think my predecessors would agree when I say that the view from the Oval Office provides a different perspective—one that only the gentlemen assembled can truly appreciate," Mr. Obama said.

"Oh, I agree," Justice said. "My point was that in order to be President of the United States, it also requires that one live with a certain amount of hypocrisy—it's unavoidable. And the mistake that you and your colleagues have made, in my view, is the attempt to make the hypocrisy something that it isn't. Each of you, but especially those scholars who have deemed some of you to be among America's greatest presidents, have lived with, and in some respects, justified the existence of hypocrisy."

"Is that why you brought us here?" Mr. Teddy Roosevelt asked. "To give us lessons on presidential hypocrisy?"

"Not exactly," Justice replied.

"What then?" Mr. Truman asked.

Justice took the men over to a large screen where they could see the events of the day playing out in real-time. They watched as protestors stormed the Capitol.

"That looks very much like the reports that I received about the storming of the Bastille in Paris around the time of my presidency," Mr. Washington said.

"It's actually the storming of your nation's Capitol," Justice replied. "This, gentlemen, is hypocrisy run amok."

"You can't place the blame of that insanity on any of us," Mr. Washington shot back.

"I wouldn't presume to indict any of you directly, but indirectly, all of you in some capacity contributed to the culmination of what you're witnessing."

"I must protest, sir!" Mr. John Adams proclaimed. "As I warned, the future was in the hands of posterity! I feared then, as we are witnessing now, they would never know how much it cost my generation to preserve their freedom! What you are showing us now appears to be the actual fruit of my concern."

"Well said, Mr. Adams, but aren't you forgetting the Alien and Seditions Acts that you signed into law in 1798? Were those not an encroachment on the First Amendment? And why are you laughing, Mr. Wilson? I might ask you the same thing about the Espionage Act of 1917?"

"It's important that you understand that the United States was at war, and, as I told Congress, the world must be made safe for democracy," President Woodrow Wilson said in response.

"Mr. Wilson, does that include ignoring the First Amendment like your predecessor, Mr. Adams? Does being president always require the ends justify the means?" Justice asked. Looking directly at Truman, Justice queried rhetorically, "Would that include the decision to use the atomic bomb?"

Before Wilson or Truman could respond, Justice immediately cut them off. "Let me guess, gentlemen, you're about to explain the unique perspective that has been entrusted in the one occupying the Oval Office. You may be right, but does that justify the long-term implications of your actions? Each of you has been quick to argue for the uniqueness of your position—no one has said, 'Well, maybe I got that one wrong.' Why is that? Could it be that you all have made peace with your particular hypocrisy?"

"I do feel, as many of my colleagues have already pointed out, you're oversimplifying the complexities of the office," Franklin Roosevelt said.

"Mr. Roosevelt, is it an oversimplification to offer that your executive order 9066, which led to Japanese internment during WWII, bore striking similarities to the treatment of German Americans during WWI under President Wilson? I believe you also served in that administration as well."

Then the presidents entered the final door. It was an empty room except for a pile of ashes on the floor. President Truman asked: "What the hell is this?" Justice told him that it was documents that were irrelevant so they were burned. No one thought much of it, but as Madison passed the debris, he noticed a sliver of paper that had not been burned—it read: "We the People." Then Madison asked, "Was that the…?"

"Yes," Justice replied in a calm voice. "It was the Constitution. I didn't think you needed it, not with justifying slavery, ignoring habeas corpus, or sanctioning the internment of innocent Americans. It seemed to be more of a document of convenience rather than a written declaration or a codified commitment to liberty and equality. At key moments, the Constitution was ignored in order to ensure its survival long-term. Maybe the hypocrisy was unavoidable, but it is the tacit agreement that each of you made when you declared: 'To the best of my ability, preserve, protect, and defend the Constitution of the United States.' Each of you has the distinction of being the temporary standard bearer of the most unique democratic form of government devised—one that depends on the ideals of liberty and equality first articulated by Mr. Jefferson in 1776. Regardless of your best intentions, the hypocrisy, or the unique perspective from the Oval Office, the daunting reality remains: whenever you made decisions that moved away from the cherished ideals of 1776, it contributes to the melee you're witnessing on January 6, 2021."

"I have had enough of this!" Lyndon Johnson cried. "How do we get out of here?"

Justice then pointed to a small hole that was barely visible, suggesting to the president that this was the only way out. Theodore Roosevelt peered through the hole and saw an open space even darker than the room they were in.

"Are you sure this is the only way out?" Roosevelt asked. "Assuming that we can squeeze through this hole, all I see is more darkness—there is nothing that guarantees I will make it back to safety. And there's no way Taft can make it through that hole!"

Then an exasperated and rotund President Taft cried out: "This is hopeless!"

"You should have paid more attention to the inscription on the gate before we entered," Liberty replied.

CHAPTER 8

The Floridita

This story was inspired by filmmaker, Ken Burns' documentary on Ernest Hemingway. The 20th century's most acclaimed writer was also one of its greatest enigmas who divided life between the extremes of his personal life and the public avatar he created to conceal the contradictions.

THE KID WAS RIGHT—that was a damn good mojito and well worth the $2 I gave him to ascertain the information of its whereabouts. I desperately wanted a second one but I had another destination of the utmost importance. Besides, two was my limit before I entered the valley of inebriation. Dusk had begun to shroud the enchanted province of Havana, and I still didn't know how to reach my exact destination.

I should have asked the kid, but he was long gone, probably splurging on his $2 windfall. I had to locate the Hotel Floridita before closing time.

I spotted an old man smoking a cigar. The tenderness he displayed cutting and lighting his cigar suggested he was the perfect person to ask. Anyone displaying such compassion to a cigar would extend similar to a traveler in need of direction.

He sat in a rocking chair outside a small store. The enjoyment of the cigar appeared to be his sole priority. The satisfaction conveyed in his body language suggested any responsibilities, pressing or otherwise, would have to wait. As was true about *Santiago* in the *Old Man and the Sea*, everything about the man in the rocking chair was old, except his eyes. Who better to tell me how to get to the Hotel Floridita than someone reminiscent of one of Hemingway's famous protagonists.

He could not speak English and there seemed to be no discernable distinction between my Spanish and Swahili. Frustrated that I did not pay more attention in my high school Spanish classes, I blurted out, "I'm never going to find Hemingway's famous watering hole."

The old man lit up, "Ernesto Hemingway! Papa! Hotel Floridita! *Si!*"

As the old man spoke, I discovered a momentary level of fluency and comprehension. I also gained an added appreciation for Ernest Hemingway and the manner he transcended the spoken word. There comes a point where America's most notable writer since Mark Twain is beyond description, characterization, or definition. And I was in Havana to find him, to talk with him, to pick his brain about the art form of writing. But my enthusiasm was concealed under the midst of whom I was truly seeking.

Was it Ernest Miller Hemingway the novelist,

foreign correspondent, short-story writer, known for his economical writing style that I sought? Or was I seeking "Papa," the avatar, the self-constructed image by Hemingway's own hand the sportsman and bullfight aficionado, overflowing with all things masculine?

The problem with the self-constructed image is that one often ignores the self-induced cannibalistic impulses until they are consumed. Moreover, it is developed for an audience that does not possess the phrase "that's enough" in its vocabulary. But in the end, it was irrelevant. Like Ahab's obsession with the white whale, I was consumed with learning more about Hemingway. It didn't matter which Hemingway I found—they were inextricably linked.

America has produced numerous writers whose style I prefer. Baldwin, Morrison, Ellison, even Hemingway's friend during his days in Paris, F. Scott Fitzgerald, are among those whose prose titillates me more than Hemingway. But it's Papa who beckons—the mystique birthed by the polarities of the flawed individual and the apotheosis of the fictionalized character he constructed.

Havana is beautiful any time of day, but at night, it is truly spectacular. It wears its history on its sleeve. Dominated by its unique Baroque and neoclassical architecture, I expected at any moment to encounter Spanish conquistadors.

The combination of being on the brink of intoxication and captivated by the ethos of Havana, I lost track of time. I wasn't sure if the Floridita would still be open by the time I arrived, let alone if Hemingway would be there. But as I turned the corner, I saw this pink pastel building. The electric sign predating the Revolution, reminiscent of a very different Havana pierced the darkness of night, reading: Floridita. Adjacent was another sign that bore Hemingway's signature.

Whether the individual or the avatar, I was about to enter the domain of one of the most important writers produced in the 20th century. Overcome by a shortness of breath, this expedition felt like a much better proposition when I asked the old man earlier for directions than actually standing at the door of the Floridita as its lights casted negligible illumination on its pink facade.

To my surprise, no one was there. No music, just a lone bartender adorning the red jacket the Floridita staff is known for. He was standing in front of a sign that was written in English. The bartender noticed that I was trying to read it, so he politely moved. It read: "The cradle of the daiquiri." I believed those were Hemingway's words.

This is part of what makes Hemingway so interesting. Whether his virtues or shortcomings, every aspect of his life was art pregnant with passion. He's not the first writer to love a drink, but he's one of few that I would make the pilgrimage to visit the location.

The bartender smiled at me, and without saying a word, quickly surmised why I was here. He subtly cut his eyes toward the end of the bar on his right, and there, in a leaning posture, stood my reason for journeying to the

Hotel Floridita. He was physically larger than I assumed and his aura more so. Above Hemingway was a photo of him with Fidel Castro.

I didn't want to be obtrusive, but I would have felt stupid sitting on the other side of the bar. I sat three bar stools away, close enough to be in his space but far enough if he wished to maintain his anonymity. But I was counting on the fact that Hemingway loved an audience.

Looking straight ahead, I ordered a mojito. Immediately, I heard a condescending laughter, bellowing from my left.

"Another goddam, touristy fucking American who took the 90-mile trek to torment me. What, no good bars in Miami?" Hemingway said.

"I don't know what you're talking about, I simply ordered a drink."

"Yeah, but you ordered a mojito at the Floridita."

"What's wrong with that?" I asked.

"If you wanted a mojito, you should have gone to Bodeguita. Instead, you're here. This place specializes in daiquiris. But I'm here and that's the point!"

Hemingway's reputation of being an insufferable oracle was on full display. But he was right... the Bodeguita was where the kid took me when I asked, 'Where could I find a good mojito?' But now I'm here in the "cradle of the Daiquiri." And I don't like daiquiris.

"Let me guess, you're another one of those aspiring writers who has come to kiss the ring of Papa? Let me tell you something, and this one is free, there is no such thing as an aspiring writer. Either you're a writer or you're not. And if you need a publishing house, literary agent, editor, or book sales to know which one you are, then it's already been answered."

I felt he was already losing patience with my presence. Why should I assume otherwise? I decided I would excuse myself and apologize for having bothered him, but he surprisingly spoke up:

"If you haven't noticed, the place will be closing soon. If you're to bore me with your meaningless drivel, the least you can do is buy me another drink."

"Why do you consider my curiosity drivel?"

"If you had something meaningful to offer the world, you would be focused on that. You wouldn't have the time or the motivation to chase me down."

"Who said I was chasing you down?"

"Because you're at the Floridita. I'm sure you noticed my signature is outside. Do you know how many people from around the world come here because this was my favorite spot? Look at the pictures on the wall, Gary Cooper, Spencer Tracy, Katharine Hepburn, Ava Gardner, Ingrid Bergman, and the others. How do you think they found this place? Me! So, yes, you're chasing me down and all I can say is: 'Get in fucking line!'"

"Well, at least allow me to introduce myself, my name is—"

He abruptly cut me off. "Your goddamn name isn't important, and you already know mine. Plus, it is unlikely I will remember it tomorrow."

"This conversation is exactly the way I thought it

would be," I said.

"How so?"

"You feeling compelled to deposit your masculine markings so that any passerby would know Papa was here!"

"What's wrong with that?"

"Nothing, I guess. But I would think that has to be exhausting."

"What?"

"Just being you!"

"But just being me is what brought you down here."

"I admit that I wanted to meet and talk with you, but it increasingly feels like a better idea in theory than in actuality."

"Aren't you a smug little son-of-a-bitch?"

"Would that make me a Martha Gellhorn redux?"

I quickly realized I had hit a nerve. Decades had passed but mentioning the name "Gellhorn" was enough to throw the great man off kilter. Were it not for the three bar stools that separated us, I probably would have been lying flat on the floor, the recipient of a Hemingway right hand across the face as he had done with others he deemed malcontents who were not impressed by his charisma.

I had suspected for some time that Hemingway's long-held animosity for Martha Gellhorn was not based on a failed marriage—he had plenty of those—but the manner that she had successfully controlled the narrative in the post-marital years.

In an attempt to intimidate me, with an added dose

of emasculation, Hemingway offered: "If you were a man, a real man, I would have knocked you on your ass for your last remark."

He was feeling defensive, so I confidently shot back, "Why? She showed up unannounced at Sloppy Joes in Key West and I showed up in a similar manner looking for you at the Floridita. I don't see the difference."

"Well, I do. You don't have long, slender legs and you're not a frigid bitch in bed. And if you are, I'm never going to find out."

"That's pretty harsh, don't you think?"

"Not harsh enough! All she wanted was to be 'Mrs. Ernest Hemingway', and since our divorce, she has portrayed herself as the helpless victim, and a group of no-nothings classified her as 'The Woman who stood up to Hemingway.'"

"Isn't that true? You pretty much had your way with Hadley, Pauline, and Mary. It seems Martha is the outlier."

A melancholy look came over his face, suggesting vulnerability, though looking in my direction, it was unclear that his words were meant for me.

"I should have never left Hadley. That's when I was the happiest, that's the one I truly loved," he said.

"Judging by your life, I would say that it has been your public image that you truly loved. And it was the contributions of Pauline and her family that led to your preeminence as a writer."

"Hadley understood me in ways that others did not. Life was simple with her," he said.

"When was the last time you were content with simple?" I asked. "You were married to Hadley when only a few outside of your writing circle knew who you were. You were not comparable to Fitzgerald at the time—you were looking up to Gertrude Stein, hoping to meet James Joyce. You had not become 'Hemingway' and that persona has proven to be more important to you than personal contentment," I said.

"I thought you came here to kiss my ass!"

"I did… or at least I thought so."

"What changed your mind?"

"You did! I never realized that under that tough uber masculine exterior was a sad insecure man."

"And I never thought I would waste so much time with another pseudo-analyst trying to figure me out! Do you know how many people have taken on that job with no success?"

"I can imagine," I said.

"No, you can't imagine. I decided not to go to college, much to my parents' chagrin. At 17, I took a job with the Kansas City Star as a cub reporter, and now you can get a fucking Ph.D. studying me! I have influenced every goddamn writer for the last 100 years. Even those poor bastards that have never read my stuff are influenced by me and don't fucking know it. I'm the Pablo Picasso of writing. Which period in Papa's grand life will we study today?"

Hemingway, overwrought with bravado, relied on it as a defense mechanism to camouflage his vulnerability. I tried to imagine him hosting a dinner party. I wondered if he treated guests, especially after a few drinks, as enemy combatants. If so, were they protected by the Geneva Convention?

"If you believe what you say, why the need for *A Moveable Feast*?" I asked.

"I don't know if you've bothered to notice, but that book still sells like frozen daiquiris in hell. Speaking of daiquiris... I thought you were going to buy me one?"

"Yes, of course!"

"Constantino," Hemingway roared. "Double, por favor! So, what type of stuff do you write?" he asked with a curiosity that could only be compared to that of a turkey at an ax convention.

"Nonfiction and fiction," I said. "Everything that I write is influenced by American history.

"Are you any good?"

"I think so!"

"Well, send me something and I will critique it!"

"Like you critiqued *From Here to Eternity*?

"That book was shit! And I was not about to lend my name to help a deserter of war get rich writing about the war he deserted."

"As I recall, Lt. Henry deserted and fled to Switzerland with Catherine Barkley in *A Farewell to Arms*."

"But I didn't desert it, that author did!"

"That author?" I asked. "Would you by any chance be referring to James Jones?"

"If you say that's his name, I will take your word for it! He didn't register high enough on my respect meter to remember his name."

I shook my head, unable to conceal my disgust at

what I perceive as a self-centered behavior. He shot back:

"I suppose you believe I should have given that traitor my support?"

"Not necessarily, but didn't the request come from Charles Scribner?"

"I don't see how that makes any difference?"

"It makes a difference because it was a personal request from a friend."

"Scribner was a friend, but does that mean I'm obligated to write a favorable review?"

"No, but were you obligated to level a vicious attack? What was in the book that required you to respond with cruel invectives? Were you protecting your legacy? Or was it a case of inane jealousy?"

Hemingway paused. He was overwhelmed by a look that suggested he was desperately seeking a response to justify his unjustifiable behavior. Fortunately, he was rescued by timing.

Constantino, who is believed to have originated the daiquiri, sat the double cocktail down in front of Hemingway. He thanked Constantino in a manner that was more than perfunctory, but rather in a way that suggested he saw his humanity. Hemingway then turned to me, grinning with a smile borrowed from the Cheshire Cat in *Alice in Wonderland*.

"You know, I have the house record for the most daiquiris consumed in a single sitting," he said.

"Is that something we should include in your obituary?" I asked. "But you never addressed my question about *A Moveable Feast*."

"I didn't know there was a question."

"If you were so confident about 'Papa's grand life', why the need to settle scores with people who had long been dead as you did with certain individuals in *A Moveable Feast*, namely Stein and Fitzgerald?"

"You don't understand... you weren't there. Gertrude Stein was jealous of my success, and Scott Fitzgerald was a great writer who became a wasted talent—weak. He was too concerned about the feelings of that crazy bitch, Zelda. You can't be a great writer if you're worried about the feelings of others."

"As I wrote in *A Moveable Feast*: 'Fitzgerald's talent was as natural as the pattern that was made by the dust on a butterfly's wings. At one time, he understood it no more than the butterfly did and he did not know when it was brushed or marred. Later, he became conscious of his damaged wings and of their construction and he learned to think and could not fly anymore because the love of flight was gone and he could only remember when it had been effortless.'"

"But when Fitzgerald had died, and for that matter, Stein, you already stood alone, at the summit of the fiction racket. You had no scores to settle," I said.

"What did Gertrude Stein know?" he asked. "What did Scott Fitzgerald know? Stein hated *Up in Michigan*. That was a groundbreaking piece that she could not have conceived in a thousand years."

"But Stein and Fitzgerald were instrumental in the development of your writing career," I said.

"That's true, but not for the reasons you think. They were not there to help me, each took credit for things they had nothing to do with. Fitzgerald said it was his idea to jettison the first two chapters of *The Sun Also Rises*. And Stein did not give me the so-called Hemingway style. I had it when I met her. So, I had to set the record straight."

"You don't find that behavior petty?"

"Doesn't matter how I find it, what matters is the truth."

"Like the version of truth you offered in the preface of *A Moveable Feast*? You wrote: 'The book might be regarded as fiction, but there is also the chance that such a book of fiction may throw some light on what is written as fact.'"

"Exactly!"

"Sounds like you're trying to have it both ways, the beneficiary by being the last man standing. Maybe you should have written a second memoir. How about *The Short Unhappy Life of Ernest Hemingway: The Perennial Victim*?"

I wasn't sure if it was the culmination of multiple daiquiris or my words. For all his self-professed machismo, his skin was as thin as wet cotton candy, and he didn't have many relationships that included the reciprocity of honesty.

"You think you've got it all figured out," he said. "You read a few of my books, and you think you know me. You don't know shit! You couldn't last a week in my world."

"Maybe not," I said. "But you're assuming I want to

be in your world."

"I know you want to be in my world or you wouldn't be here now. But you don't have what it takes—nobody does."

"That's a rather pompous declaration," I said.

"It's not pompous if it's true! Do you know what separates me from every other fucking writer?"

"I have my thoughts, but I'm sure you're about to tell me," I said.

"I was there! How many of my writings, newspaper articles, short stories, or novels were created without my being there? I'm trying to always get the actual feeling across, not to just depict life or criticize it, but to actually make it alive. So, when you've read something by me, you actually experience the thing. Ralph Ellison, the Negro writer, said, 'When Hemingway describes something in print, believe him; he's been there.'

"Then he began speaking in the third person:

"When Hemingway writes, you don't just get his voice, but you also get his eyes, and his eyes put you there. You are at the running of the bulls and watching bullfights up close in *The Sun Also Rises*, involved in the Spanish Civil War in *For Whom the Bell Tolls*, and you're in the boat with Santiago in *The Old Man and the Sea*. I could go on, but no other bastard can do it the way I can."

"But why the need to constantly remind the rest of us of what we already know?"

He quickly responded:

"The critics took delight in telling the world when they

thought my latest book wasn't as good as the previous one. They organize their lives around predetermining my literary obituary. All the critics who could not make their reputations by discovering you are hoping to make them by predicting your approaching impotence, failure, and general drying up of natural juices."

"Why does that matter? You had books that critics didn't particularly like that still sold well. Aren't readers the ultimate critics?"

"Everyone wants to see the man on top fail," he said. "Every book I write is like a heavyweight championship fight. Will Papa defend his crown or will he lose to some upstart?"

Sticking with his boxing metaphor, I said, "But no American writer has ever held the title as long as you."

"But in my case, everyone pretends to be some sort of Hemingway expert! Hell, I'm not a Hemingway expert."

"But you created a fallacy of who and what Hemingway is for public consumption, why are you surprised everyone thinks they know you? Isn't that what you wanted... some version of you that you created?"

"Whenever I write something," he said. "Everyone assumes I belong to their side. Look at the heat I took for writing about the cruelties of war in *For Whom the Bell Tolls*! Some thought I should have condemned the fascists while extolling only the virtues of the loyalists as if the realities of war can be condensed so neatly. Everyone loved me for my uncanny ability to see and then they rebuked me for writing down what I saw."

"It's really difficult to feel for you," I said. "How many books have you sold not because they were good, but because the name Ernest Hemingway adorned the cover?"

Bristling in a manner that suggested the conversation was reaching finality, he said:

"You couldn't carry my burdens for an hour! Just because you've written a few things, you're not in my league! No one is! Just as I told Gellhorn, they will still be reading my stuff long after the worms are done with you. So, the best you, or anyone else can be is some goddamn sycophant."

I assumed the daiquiris he consumed had the floor because he felt compelled to once again remind me that I didn't measure up to him. There was consternation in his voice that combined certainty and uncertainty. Hemingway the individual, a flawed genius, was in tension with the global creation that he and much of the world mythologized to the point his last name was all that was required to know exactly whom one was referring to. I stood transfixed by the glimpses of vulnerability—even his willingness to wrestle with the warring factions of the "two Hemingways" endeared me.

But in the end, he had become a permanent captive to his public creation, the embodiment of *Frankenstein's* monster. He found irredeemable solace in having us believe he was indeed a composite of so many of the characters he told us about in print. It was buttressed by a lifestyle created largely by his hand. Whether it was the wounded war veteran, the embattled war correspondent, big game hunter, deep-sea fisherman, bullfight connoisseur, or brawler, his public persona offered a smorgasbord of masculine delights. But it proved to be a *Faustian* bargain. Even the role as America's most prolific writer of the 20th century became a side hustle, deferential to the image he spent more than three decades cultivating. Hemingway's understanding of the human condition remains unparalleled. But the price exacted for that skill would ultimately become his inability to know himself.

Great writing is a memorable journey not bound by other qualifications. Reading anything by Hemingway, I didn't care where I was going or the ultimate destination—I was thankful for the voyage. With bolstered confidence and compassion, I was prepared to ask more probing questions, but Constantino grabbed me by the arm to get my attention, "Señor," he said softly. "We're closed!"

I turned abruptly, somewhat startled. I apologized to Constantino for being unaware of the time, then paid for my drinks and walked out. As I got to the door, I turned once more to gaze at the bronze statue of Hemingway at the end of the bar—a permanent fixture at the Floridita.

CHAPTER 9

Alone

Mental health impacts our emotional, psychological, and social well-being. It affects how we think, feel, and act. It can also determine the manner that we handle stress. Alone reflects my ongoing mental health challenges.

SOLITUDE IS MY life partner. It has not been a relationship defined by decades of bliss, more like a long-term dysfunctional entanglement. Don't misunderstand me; it hasn't been without its euphoric moments. There are times when the isolation takes a toll on my psyche. Those are the times when I feel an intense desire to withdraw, and, frankly, I would put an end to this whole life journey were it not for my lack of courage.

Given the choice between sustaining meaningful relationships or my solitude, I always choose the latter. One may very well conclude, and they would be correct when factoring mind, body, and soul, that solitude is the only relationship where I've been completely faithful. I have sought counseling. I have aired my differences, only to have solitude remind me of things they have done to make me a better person. But after three consecutive sleepless nights, I decided to confront my demon head-on.

2:00 AM

"Why won't you let me sleep?" I asked.

"Look at the creativity I've fostered in your soul— creativity that others have benefitted," Solitude exclaimed. Adding, "I have done for you what heroin did for Charlie Parker, without the corrosive side effects."

"Ah, but there were side effects," I shot back. "You created a dependency that is difficult to shake. You become evil when you are jealous, undermining every meaningful relationship that I've ever had. You're so seductive, even when I tell someone that you're behind it, they find it difficult to comprehend such influence over another is possible. Plus, heroin killed Charlie Parker and it destroyed countless others."

"Well, I thought we understood each other."

"You understand me much better than I comprehend your existence. You live in my head rent-free. But it never seems to be enough."

"That's because you choose to conveniently ignore the closing line from the song, *Hotel California*, 'You can check out anytime you like, but you can never leave'."

"Damn, you! I want some normalcy. I'm sick of these dark clouds permeating my soul."

"Normalcy is so overrated. Do you think Lincoln, Van Gough, or Miles Davis had normalcy? Not that I'm comparing you to those incomparable geniuses, but the dark clouds you so bemoan hold the keys to your creativity, which is incongruent with normalcy. Furthermore, you like being in your head. Whether you wish to admit it or not, you need me."

"That's a stretch."

"Oh, I wouldn't say so. How much of your creativity occurred while mingling with others? While you're masquerading as an extrovert, extolling every ounce of energy to hide that you would rather be in a corner comforted by me, how creative were you then? Was it not more often in your isolation, alone with me, when your creativity flourished?"

"Are you suggesting that I couldn't function without your morose bullshit?"

"I believe I just struck a nerve."

"Don't flatter yourself."

"You're the one resorting to expletives in order to overlook the obvious."

"What obvious are you referring to?"

"I was hoping it wouldn't be necessary to bring this up. About 20 years ago, didn't you take medication to correct your 'imbalance'?"

"You already know the answer."

"Why did you stop?"

"You know that answer as well."

"I do know, but it seems you have forgotten. Why don't you humor me by saying it out loud?"

"I stopped taking the medication because I found it difficult to…"

"Why did you stop? Were you about to say you

found it difficult to be creative on the medication? If that's what you were about to say, and we both know it was, is that not an admission that you need me?"

"Now that truly is some bullshit. Did you really just take credit for my creativity?"

"Is there any other way to say it?"

"How about it's my creativity, not yours?"

"Okay, why don't you start taking the pills tomorrow, I will be gone, and let's see how creative you'll be?"

"That's a non-sequitur. One has nothing to do with the other. Your existence in my head that has led to my being alone, unable to sustain meaningful relationships of any variety, started long before I tapped into my creative side."

"Maybe so, but I'm still taking credit for your creativity."

"Whatever. We're done here."

"No worries. I will be here when you wake up."

Three hours later...

"Are you still here?"

"Of course I am... who else is here when you're all alone?"

"I am alone because of you."

"No, my friend. You're alone because you don't know how to coexist with my reality."

"Aren't we beaming with self-confidence this morning?

"One of us has to, and I certainly can't depend on

you to take the self-confident lead, at least not where I'm concerned."

"I don't want you around."

"That's what you say. Are you sure?"

"Isn't that a stupid question? Yes, I want you gone!"

"But if I leave, you will be all alone. That's pretty pathetic to live in isolation and not have it to comfort you."

"Is that what you call this? Comfort? Do you call the anxiety that I live with comfort?"

"That's exactly what it is. Without me, you would be completely alone.

"I'm completely alone now."

"Isn't that your choice?"

"Sometimes, but you know it's more complicated than that. It literally becomes difficult to breathe at times. I push people away, some that I really care about because I can't stand to be around myself, let alone anyone else. I've come to expect that no one will understand, and if they see that side, they won't like it. In fact, when they do see that side, they don't like me."

"So, I'm to blame because once people get to know you, they think you're a selfish jerk?"

"No, I've got to take responsibility for my behavior, but you don't make it any easier."

"That's why I never try to provide you with useless responses when you're feeling that way. I don't tell you to just snap out of it, provide you with some alternative activity of my choosing under the guise of making you feel better, or offer that you're being selfish because you never ask me when I'm feeling down like others do. Like it or not, I'm the one that truly knows you as you are. You hide from everyone else."

"So, you want an accommodation award for further driving me into the rabbit hole of your creation?"

"I do feel there are times when you don't appreciate my contribution to your life."

"I can't wait to hear about this."

"Without me, you wouldn't know how to set boundaries. I have heard you say you cannot afford to place your mental health in a secondary position. Do you know how many people in this world wished they knew how to establish boundaries like that?"

"Here's where I thank you for playing and inform you that you get a set of steak knives that no one has ever heard of as a lovely parting gift."

"Okay, I will leave."

"Is this the Jedi mind trick or something? We both know you're not going anywhere."

"That's only because you need me. But if you want me to go, just say the word and I'm gone."

"Like I'm supposed to believe that. Over the decades, I've asked you to leave many times and you've ignored my request. Why should I believe you're willing to acquiesce now?"

"Because you need to be taught a lesson!"

"A lesson?"

"Yes, a lesson. A lesson about who's really in charge here. So, if you want me to leave, just say the word. But you have to mean it. You can't merely mouth it, it must come from the heart!"

"I've made it clear numerous times that I want you

out of my life."

"Then say it."

"Why do I have to prove it to you?"

"You don't, but you have to prove it to yourself, and I don't think you can do that."

"Ha! Haughtiness runs amok, I see."

"Then say it. Tell me that you want me gone permanently."

"You and I both know it doesn't work like that."

"Then take your stupid pills. Find that chemical balance that you allegedly long for. See how much peace will be added to your life."

"I hate you. I really hate you."

"Hate has got nothing to do with it. Plus, to hate me is to hate you. Well, that does raise another possibility."

"What possibility might that be?"

"Oh, I think you know."

"No, I really don't know."

"My God, how is it possible for you to be so pathetic? You want me to leave, so you say, in order to frolic in some Shangri-La existence. When I offer that you should just say the word and I will leave, you hesitate. You won't take the pills because you know that would result in you being a fucking greeter at Walmart for the remainder of your pitiful life, using your culinary skills to come up with creative ways to eat Top Ramen. Then I suggest another way out and you feign stupidity."

"There's another option."

"What, pray tell?"

"I can call your bluff."

"You think I'm bluffing?"

"No, but you're not as much in control as you would like me to believe."

"Are you sure about that?"

"I'm certainly willing to find out."

"Do you know how many so-called artists are part of my collateral damage over the centuries? Tolstoy, Hemmingway, Fitzgerald, and O'Keefe are all part of my distinguished coalition. I can't tell you how many have bowed at my altar. Hell, I should be getting royalties from the Van Gough estate. Show me a great work of art, however defined, and chances are my influence is also there. As you can see, your feeble declaration of self-determination is meaningless to me."

"But it means something to me."

"I'm not going anywhere."

"I'm not either. I accept that you're the 800-lb. gorilla on my back that will show up at inopportune moments. You are particularly disruptive in my personal relationships. But none of that defines me. You don't get credit for my creativity. It happens in spite of your presence, certainly not because of it."

"Should I stand and applaud that soliloquy?"

"Do whatever you desire. I just want you out of my life."

"People in hell want ice water and central air conditioning."

"Just get out! Get out of my head and take your unwanted anxiety with you."

"Okay, I'll leave. Frankly, it's no fun to be around you when you're full of your own strength. But guess what?"

"What?"

"I'll be back."

"Don't be so sure."

"I'm sure."

"What makes you so sure?"

"Because I'm the only permanent relationship in your life."

It felt liberating standing up to Solitude that way. But I also knew Solitude would make good on the promise to return. With that, I felt a twinge of anxiety once again penetrating my soul.

PART
II

NONFICTION ESSAYS

On the surface, it would appear this collection of nonfiction essays is held together by America's ongoing racial tension. Though there is an undeniable racial thread, ultimately, these essays reflect America's methodical drift away from its civic virtue of liberty and equality. It is an uncharted destination relying on a demagnetized moral compass for guidance.

Invariably the subject of race invokes the reflexive question: Is America a racist nation? My own view holds, assuming one can ascertain a common definition on race, racism, or racist, the question is too opaque to capture the totality that is the American experiment. But race and racial capitalism have played indispensible roles in the formation of the empire known as America.

Just as Henry Highland Garnet observed in 1843, the difficulty that enslaved African descendants faced in their quest for a liberating exodus, "The Pharaohs were on both sides of the blood red waters," racism works in a similar manner. Its toxins are pernicious to the victim and victimizer. Any discussions about racism are invariably presented as a stand-alone subject. I view it as a tragic obfuscation, a convenient roadblock, ensconced in fear, assumption, and reactionary discourse that keeps the nation beholden to a macabre arrested development, unable to fulfill the vision articulated in the Declaration of Independence. It is important to underscore the American project began with an inordinate amount of the populous was disenfranchised, regardless of race or gender. But race has been America's pervasive smokescreen that prohibits the nation from reaching its potential based on its original commitments. Race forces us to helplessly stand proxy for the hamster on the treadmill. It is the gold standard for civic immaturity. It is a path that can only lead to implosion from within.

The Reemergence
of the White Male Landowner

When the nation was founded, the only individuals that possessed full citizenship was the white male landowner. This meant, depending on the statistics, as many as 84 % of Americans, regardless of their race and gender, were disenfranchised—a contradictory practice for a nation that expressly stated all were created equal. With rollbacks to the 1965 Voting Rights Act, state legislation designed to systematically make voting more difficult, and overturning Roe V. Wade, the white male landowner motif has returned, upgraded to adapt to 21st century customs.

SEVERAL YEARS AGO, I taught a course on the Declaration of Independence, and an African American student challenged the significance of the document. He said the Declaration, along with the Constitution, were irrelevant because they were written exclusively for white male landowners.

I immediately had all the students stand. I said, "If you are a person of color, sit down!" Then I asked all the women to sit down. This left three white males standing. I then said, "If you don't own property, sit down."

With only one student standing, I told the class that the initial observation that prompted the exercise was accurate but not precise. It was accurate in that the original beneficiaries of America's democratic-republican largesse were indeed white male landowners. But nowhere does white male landowner appear in the document outlining America's public morality.

The voting franchise, and therefore, full citizenship adopted by many of the 13 colonies, were based on specific race, gender, and wealth considerations. The result disenfranchised roughly 84% of America's 18th-century population. Those not originally included have sought to make America's words and deeds synonymous through the long and arduous trek toward the amorphous "more perfect union" that leads to full citizenship.

The Constitution in its original form placed the nation in moral tension with itself, granting constitutional legitimacy to the institution of slavery while committing to the Enlightenment virtues of liberty and equality in the Declaration of Independence.

In addition to a war for independence, it required a civil war, several constitutional amendments, landmark Supreme Court decisions, and the valor by a portion of the 84% and their descendants who were not originally included to redefine the "we" in "We the People" to something more inclusive than its restrictive origins.

In the 21st century, the "white male landowner" has reemerged as a metaphor that depicts the systematic rollback of hard-fought rights for those originally left out of America's commitments to liberty and equality. Just as America's 18th-century gentry class, whose founding precepts coalesced around race, gender, and assets as the criteria for full citizenship, the nation's current trajectory has them on pace to be the last ones standing in the onslaught of regressive policies that undermine the progress made to make the nation congruent with its original propositions.

From recent Supreme Court decisions to the fantasia known as the "culture wars", America is increasingly becoming engulfed in a cocoon that normalizes "othering." By 2020, the 6-3 conservative majority on the Supreme Court was made up of five of the six justices appointed by presidents that did not win the popular vote in the General Election. It reflects the inverted order of a phrase first attributed to Alexis de Tocqueville— *tyranny of the majority*.

Tyranny of the Minority

America's trajectory, in spite of its lofty language, has always erred on the side of its small, but well-heeled faction. The 21st century rollbacks to civil rights on the basis of fairness, equality, changing times, and newly discovered enlightenment are rationales to overtly return to the preeminence of the white male landowner or *tyranny of the minority*.

In February 2022, a leaked Supreme Court opinion, written by Justice Samuel Alito, placed the country on notice that the Court would overturn Roe v. Wade, and a woman's constitutional right to an abortion. Alito offered the right to abortion was not "deeply rooted in the nation's history." It is a fascinating statement that paradoxically substantiates its claim by not being deeply rooted in the nation's history.

Equality, as part of America's civic virtue, was introduced in 1776, but it wasn't until 1868 with the ratification of the Fourteenth Amendment that it was expressly stated in the Constitution. Fifty years after the Fifteenth Amendment that prohibited voting restrictions based on race, women still needed the passage of the Nineteenth Amendment, and as many legal scholars opine, it was only with the 1965 Voting Rights Act that equality became ubiquitous. At what point was this cherished value deeply rooted in the nation's history?

The argument to take away a right that has existed for half a century is justified by a subjective historical analysis supported by a veneer of legal coating that hardly seems consistent with the ethos of the American experiment. Moreover, wouldn't Alito's opinion, if taken literally, suggest the only group whose rights that are deeply rooted in the nation's history would be those of the white male landowner.

Privacy

Justice Alito's leaked opinion went well beyond the Court striking down Roe; it was a manifesto against the right to privacy. Alito, who self-identifies as a "practical originalist," wrote the decision to overturn Roe as if the Constitution could be judiciously understood through the application of a series of closed-ended questions.

It seems in Justice Alito's constitutional worldview, if a right is not expressly stated, in this case, the right to privacy, it does not exist. Justice Alito would be correct if the American experiment, and more broadly, the human condition were a linear odyssey. Though privacy may not specifically be mentioned, its tenets are woven into the fabric of our constitutional inheritance.

The First Amendment protects free association—the government cannot regulate who one associates with. The Fourth Amendment protects against unreasonable searches and seizures. The government cannot burst into one's home and rifle through one's property without probable cause. Law enforcement must not violate the individual's reasonable expectation of privacy. The Fifth Amendment protects against self-incrimination—the government cannot force an individual to divulge private affairs. And for those of an archaic mindset, even the Third Amendment, which prohibits the government from forcing individuals from quartering troops, is a protection of privacy.

This is a portion of the rationale the Court used in the landmark 1965 case of Griswold v. Connecticut, which protects a woman's right to use contraception. It was in Griswold, which provided the basis for Roe, that the Court established the right to privacy was contained in the penumbra of rights embedded in the aforementioned amendments, as well as the Ninth and Fourteenth Amendments.

Moreover, the opinion offered by Alito is constructed as if the Ninth Amendment were non-existent. The Ninth Amendment states: "The enumeration in the Constitution, of certain rights, shall not be construed to deny or disparage others retained by the people."

Though the Ninth Amendment does not protect a certain right, such as speech or due process, it advances the scope of the Constitution beyond what was originally committed to parchment.

As Justice Arthur Goldberg opined in Griswold:

> *"Since 1791 [the Ninth Amendment] has been a basic part of the Constitution which we are sworn to uphold. To hold that a right so basic and fundamental and so deep-rooted in our society as the right of privacy in marriage may be infringed because that right is not guaranteed in so many words by the first eight amendments to the Constitution is to ignore the Ninth Amendment and to give it no effect whatsoever."*

The manner that Justice Alito's leaked opinion was argued, marriage equality (Obergell v. Hodges) and consensual sex (Lawrence v. Texas) as well as our understanding of privacy could be vacated because they are not "deeply rooted in the nation's history."

More Perfect Union

In *Shelby County v. Holder* the Court ruled in 2013 that Section 5 of the Voting Rights Act was unenforceable. Section 5 froze election practices or procedures in certain states until the new procedures approved by the Justice Department, known as "preclearance." This meant that voting changes in states that had previously conducted voter suppression during the Jim Crow era, must have the approval of the Justice Department to modify their voting procedures.

Rather than citing case law, Chief Justice John Roberts, writing for the majority, offered more of a sociological analysis for striking down section 5:

> *"In assessing the 'current need' for a preclearance system that treats States differently from one another today, that history cannot be ignored. During that time, largely because of the Voting Rights Act, voting tests were abolished, disparities in voter registration and turnout due to race were erased, and African Americans attained political office in record numbers."*

The Voting Rights Act of 1965 connects dark moments in our nation's history. It is reflective of a time when the idea of liberty and equality was a secondary consideration as it applied to black Americans dating back to the nation's founding. Several states previously under Section 5 quickly moved to make voting more difficult, along with several states not bound previously by preclearance restrictions.

If citizenship did not become a reality for all Americans until the 1965 Voting Rights Act, might one posit it is voter suppression that is deeply rooted in the nation's history? In this context, should the Shelby County decision be viewed as merely correcting a 48-year wrong?

The result of a centuries-long quest to move closer to that "more perfect union" has created anxiety among many whites. To portray someone of a different race, gender, and sexual orientation as outside the mainstream grants permission to view their humanity through the lens of subjectivity. The preposterous becomes believable when the subject is deemed "other." Critical Race Theory is transformed from an intellectual discipline taught in law schools into a preschool indoctrination program that primes white children to grow up with the burden of historical guilt and inferiority.

What's really at stake is a temporary injunction filed to block social transformation under terms established by the long-held Racial Contract. Taken from the book possessing the same title, authored by former Northwestern University professor Charles Mills, the Racial Contract assumes the traditional European social contract consisting of moral and political theories championed by individuals such as Thomas Hobbes, Jacque Rousseau, and Immanuel Kant was silent on matters of race and ethnicity. The Racial Contract fills in this gap through implicit and explicit understandings that maintain the ideal of white supremacy. Because white supremacy falls large under the jurisdiction of the white male landowner motif, it requires the term race/racism be expanded to denote a process of "othering." Beyond its traditional skin color definition, race/racism includes those viewed by the dominant culture as "other" based on gender, class, sexuality, religion, culture nationality, and age.

Doing the Bidding of the Gentry Class

Many Republican elected officials have hitched their

political futures to the ability to cast some group of Americans as outside the mainstream. Using the toxins of fear, they have replaced the immediate concerns that most Americans hold with abstract notions that reinforce the belief that the group in question represents an existential threat.

On the surface, they may appear to be different issues, but the attacks on voting rights, rollbacks on abortion rights, and denial of LGBT equality, along with the potential threats to other civil liberties are inextricably linked. This is simply a refurbished packaging of an old argument that seeks the preservation of power by championing an inadequate status quo.

It is, therefore, useless for those left of center politically to wonder why many low-income whites seemingly vote against their economic self-interests. The cynical playbook has now recast the priories so that the perceived threats to being white has gone from a conspiracy theory to a hate-induced orthodoxy known as "replacement theory," rendering economic self-interests secondary.

Replacement theory holds that through immigration, interracial marriage, integration, and violence, white people are being disenfranchised. The United States has yet to reach the level of Hungary, where replacement theory is dominant. Migrants in Hungary are reportedly treated cruelly at the border. LGBTQ individuals have been deemed as a threat to the Hungarian birth rate as the country pushes for women to assume traditional roles as homemakers and mothers.

In America, replacement theory possesses two strands—violent and nonviolent. The violent strand was witnessed in May 2022 as an 18-year-old white male killed 13 people in Buffalo. His uncovered manifesto revealed his devotion to replacement theory orthodoxy and his fears of "white genocide." But it is the nonviolent actors that may ultimately prove to be a greater threat to American democracy.

The nonviolent strand may present the more insidious option. Though largely vocally silent, it simmers in the same caldron of antipathy and fear. It supports "meaningful-meaningless" political gestures of othering. It supports politicians that find Critical Race Theory in math textbooks that pass laws to make voting and abortion more difficult. Such gestures are "meaningful" to supporters because the rollbacks convey the perception of normalcy being restored in America, but ultimately, they are meaningless when it comes to making life better. Thus, the nonviolent strand has made a Faustian bargain forgoing the possibility of economic progress for the belief and satisfaction that some group(s) (people of color, women, immigrants of color, the LGBTQ community, and others) will be harmed more than them.

Both strands are merely the unwitting centurions that protect the gentry class from close scrutiny. Possessing a long historical legacy, they fought in the War for Independence as well as both sides in the Civil War. They were also the public face of Jim Crow segregation—they opposed women's suffrage and equality for the LGBTQ community, attacked strikebreakers during labor disputes, all the while protecting the interests of the gentry class.

Perhaps the most sinister legacy that the original white male landowners bequeathed to future generations was to view America's civic virtue of liberty and equality through a subjective lens. Seeing themselves as aboriginal citizens, they placed restrictions on the ubiquitous declaration "All men are created equal" so that it initially applied only to their race, gender, and economic-based fraternity. Historically, the only path for change available to those originally excluded from the civic virtue has been to believe in the concepts to a greater degree than the artisans of American democracy and their descendants. The latter view their role in the 21st century as to block progress that moves the nation closer to "We the people" opting instead for an illiberal democracy reminiscent of Hungary, Russia, and China.

We stand at the crossroads of warring internal factions. One rooted in courage and backed by the historical evidence that the American narrative can change without fundamentally changing its basic composition. The other, immersed in fear, pursues the illogical path that a regressive society is not open to the ideas of progress. And for this reason, the "white male landowner" has reemerged as a metaphor to assume his rightful place, first established formally in 1787.

What to the American Slave is Your Fourth of July?

During America's annual Fourth of July festivities, many cite a portion of Frederick Douglass' July 5, 1852 address that begins: "What to the American Slave is Your Fourth of July?" This passage is used to justify those historically on the underside of American democracy to see the Fourth of July celebrations, and subsequently, the Declaration of Independence that it is based as unrelated to their lived experience.

THE THREE ELEMENTS required for great oratory are ethos, logos, and pathos. Ethos is establishing one's authority to speak on the subject; logos represents the logical argument of one's point, and pathos is the attempt to emotionally influence an audience. With the aforementioned as the standard, Frederick Douglass' July 5, 1852 address in Rochester, NY qualifies for admittance in the pantheon of great American oratory. But its greatness can only be realized when taken in totality rather than opting for the a la carte manner, pervasive in American public discourse, designed to oversimplify more so than enlighten.

The life of Douglass is one of the most improbable in the American narrative. Douglass went from being enslaved to being one of the nation's most eloquent abolitionist spokespersons. Douglass, the abolitionist, orator, and statesman, was instrumental in America, moving closer to the illusive "more perfect union." But Douglass' greatness, like other Americans of similar distinction, is buried under the historical convenience of sweeping generalizations. His July 5 speech serves as Exhibit A.

Ethos

If ethos is establishing one's authority to speak on the subject, Douglass' journey that began enslaved to speaking in his adopted hometown of Rochester on the 76th anniversary of the signing of the Declaration of Independence, provided him with unparalleled competence. Douglass' eloquence and erudition made it difficult for many whites, especially in the South to accept that he was born into slavery on the Eastern Shore of the Chesapeake Bay in Talbot County, Maryland. His legacy is a paradoxical contribution to the greatness of the American narrative. His mere presence on any American stage, armed with acumen and eloquence, embodied the absurdity of a nation embracing the concept of owning people while establishing its foundational precepts on liberty and equality.

Douglass' worldview not only included his time spent in Great Britain and Ireland, but also a lived perspective from both sides of the Mason Dixon line. For Douglass, "Life, liberty, and the pursuit of happiness" was not merely part of the most memorable phrase in the American lexicon, it represented the polarities of his journey—polarities that honed his perspective. Douglass' lived experience allowed him to simultaneously hold

American virtue and vices in a delicate balancing act in a manner unaccustomed to many in attendance during his Rochester remarks. The most strident abolitionist was forced to heed Douglass' viewpoint that included intimate knowledge of chains and the sting of the whip.

Douglass was not the first, nor the last, to use the Dec-laration of Independence to point out America's hypocritical practices. Thirty-two years earlier, abolitionist, William Lloyd Garrison, would use the Independence Day celebration to critique the paradox that had saddled the nation:

"Every Fourth of July, our Declaration of Independence is produced, with a sublime indignation, to set forth the tyranny of the mother country, and to challenge the admiration of the world. But what a pitiful detail of grievances does this document present, in comparison with the wrongs which our slaves endure! In the one case, it is hardly the plucking of a hair from the head; in the other, it is the crushing of a live body on the wheel—the stings of the wasp contrasted with the tortures of the Inquisition. Before God, I must say, that such a glaring contradiction as exists between our creed and practice the annals of six thousand years cannot parallel. In view of it, I am ashamed of my country. I am sick of our unmeaning declamation in praise of liberty and equality; of our hypocritical cant about the unalienable rights of man."

Garrison's strident remarks appeared to be rooted in the approach offered by John the Baptist. Douglass was more inclined to offer words consistent with the teachings of Jesus. His appearance in Rochester, before uttering a single word, spoke to those in attendance, as did Jesus in Luke 4:18, to "let the oppressed go free."

Logos

Douglass' authority rooted in his lived experience and intellectual heft, provided the gateway for his central point: The bodies of the enslaved are the tangible proof that America had yet to live up to its ideals. Such assertions could be made in the 21st century, but in 1852, it was a stark contradiction in that 13 years after Douglass gave his remarks it would require more than 600,000 lives to move the nation closer to its original commitments.

Douglass' improbable journey from bondage to freedom was beyond the imagination of Harriet Beecher Stowe, whose groundbreaking, anti-slavery novel, Uncle Tom's Cabin, was also released in 1852. It is doubtful that many in attendance, prior to hearing Douglass' speech, contemplated looking out on the Chesapeake Bay, as he was forced to do as a young man, their physical movements confined by the absurdities of enslavement, believing against all facts to the contrary that slavery was not the end point of their destiny.

To have one's movement curtailed by laws that rendered those of African descent inferior stood in stark contrast to the nation's commitments. The nation pursued a perilous journey pregnant with flawed rationale and compromises in order to co-exist with the institution of slavery. Though compromise has long been a hallmark of American democracy, there can be no agreed-upon middle ground when the primary issue is human dignity.

Early in the speech, Douglass states:

> *"This, for the purpose of this celebration, is the 4th of July. It is the birthday of your National Independence, and of political freedom. This, to you, is what the Passover was to the emancipated people of God. It carries your minds back to the day, and to the act of your great deliverance, and to the signs and to the wonders associated with that act and that day. This celebration also marks the beginning of another year of your national life, and reminds you that the Republic of America is now 76 years old."*

In this passage, Douglass uses "your" five times to distinguish between the cause for celebration and those toiling in bondage and dehumanization. Douglass used this literary technique more than 100 times in his 10,000-word address. Buttressing his remarks by demonstrating a searing knowledge of America's 76-year-old odyssey, Douglass' words are accompanied by a subliminal taunt as he dared those hearing his uncomfortable analysis for the first time to challenge its legitimacy.

Douglass reminds the audience, "The evil that men do, lives after them, the good is oft' interred with their bones." For Douglass, American hypocrisy was not denoted by an asterisk that required the reader to search the endnotes—it was a portion of the thesis statement originally penned in invisible ink.

Pathos

If pathos is defined as the attempt to emotionally influence an audience, then Douglass' understanding of American history, coupled with his use of the rhetorical question offers a powerful illustration.

Douglass offers:

> *"What, to the American slave, is your 4th of July? I answer; a day that reveals to him, more than all other days in the year, the gross injustice and cruelty to which he is the constant victim."*

John Adams, who was a member of the five-person committee that drafted the Declaration, believed July 2 is the date America declared its independence from Great Britain. Here are Adams' thoughts about the place July 2 would hold in the American narrative:

"[Independence Day] will be the most memorable Epocha, in the History of America. I am apt to believe that it will be celebrated, by succeeding Generations, as the great anniversary Festival... It ought to be solemnized with Pomp and Parade with shews, Games, Sports, Guns, Bells, Bonfires and Illuminations from one End of this continent to the other from this Time forward forever more.

"The Continental Congress declared its freedom from Great Britain on July 2, 1776, when it voted to approve a resolution submitted by delegate Richard Henry Lee of Virginia, declaring "That these United

Colonies are, and of right ought to be, free and independent States, that they are absolved from all allegiance to the British Crown, and that all political connection between them and the State of Great Britain is, and ought to be, totally dissolved."

After voting for independence on July 2, the Continental Congress then needed to draft a document explaining the move to the public. The original committee that drafted the declaration, per Congress' request, took an additional two days to articulate the agreed-upon edits. Congress approved the actual Declaration of Independence on July 4. The July 4 date that appears at the top of the document is actually the date the Declaration with approved edits were signed.

Though not worthy of revision, it does reflect early stages of American commercialism in the pursuit of splendor that overshadowed historical accuracy. It has contributed to its irrelevance that many feel in the 21st century. But this minor discrepancy is also noted in Douglass' Rochester speech.

The moral ramifications of a nation committed to liberty and equality, but allowing human bondage to persist could not be assuaged by emotional appeals alone. It required an understanding of American history that dwelled below the surface. Like Martin Luther King would do a century later, Douglass held a mirror of moral self-reflection for the nation to uncomfortably gaze at. He saw the jingoistic festivities that marked July 4, 1776 to be incongruent with the nation's actual history

"What to the American Slave is Your Fourth of July?" is an often-quoted passage, resurrected annually around America's July 4 commemoration. It serves as the historical gold standard for those that see contemporary celebrations of the nation's birth to be much ado about nothing. Using the power of Douglass' words, the emphasis he places on "Your 4th of July" denotes a holiday pregnant with paradox—a nation that originally bestowed full citizenship to no more than 25% of the population (white male landowners) remained unable to reconcile its inglorious past. But it is also within the pathos of Douglass' remarks where those that cite a portion as the persuasive device to disavow America's Fourth of July celebration are guilty of a similar type of oversimplification.

It is difficult to refute Douglass' critique that a nation (North and South), commemorating its birth built on the immortal words of life, liberty, and the pursuit of happiness, systematically participating in racial capitalism was the height of hypocrisy, thereby meaningless to those victimized by its macabre practices.

Douglass laments:

"To him (the enslaved), your celebration is a sham; your boasted liberty, an unholy license; your national greatness, swelling vanity; your sounds of rejoicing are empty and heartless; your denunciation of tyrants, brass fronted impudence; your shouts of liberty and equality, hollow mockery; your prayers and hymns, your sermons and thanksgivings, with all your religious parade and solemnity, are, to Him, mere bombast, fraud,

deception, impiety, and hypocrisy-a thin veil to cover up crimes which would disgrace a nation of savages. There is not a nation on the earth guilty of practices more shocking and bloody than are the people of the United States, at this very hour."

A common rebuttal to the aforementioned statement is to offer slavery was a global phenomenon, not exclusive to America. While this is a literal truism, it requires that one ignores the high bar America set when it proclaimed independence from Great Britain. Per the preamble of the Declaration of Independence, America made liberty and equality the cornerstones of its new experiment. By boldly proclaiming that the people could govern themselves, America took two centuries of Enlightenment thinking, expanded the ideas originally crafted in the Magna Carta, 500 years earlier as the basis for its secession.

It is also this portion of Douglass' speech that contemporary proponents use to justify commingling the Fourth of July celebrations with the Declaration of Independence. Douglass' critique was based on the empty calories of the July 4 celebration, not the document that spawned it. As he stated in the same speech:

"Fellow Citizens, I am not wanting in respect for the fathers of this republic. The signers of the Declaration of Independence were brave men. They were great men too—great enough to give fame to a great age." By commingling the Fourth of July

celebrations with the Declaration of Independence is to remain, albeit in a reactionary posture, in the same unproductive paradigm that it seeks to disprove.

Douglass defined the Declaration of Independence as "the ring-bolt to the chain of your nation's destiny; so, indeed, I regard it." Adding, "The principles contained in that instrument are saving principles. Stand by those principles, be true to them on all occasions, in all places, against all foes, and at whatever cost."

Critiquing the hackneyed manner of America's July 4 celebration by cherry-picking a portion of one of the greatest examples of oratory in American history further cheapens the debate. Douglass' words challenge us in this contemporary age to hold in tension America's promise and hypocrisy. Douglass was not tethered to what artisans of the document may have "intended". His focus was the principles articulated.

Has it not been those on the underside of America's stated commitments that used those principles to help the nation, albeit slowly, find its moral compass? They've borne the responsibility to hold those founding principles dear, while the status quo has historically possessed the luxury to take a more cavalier approach. Through the American narrative, valiant foot soldiers were undeterred that Thomas Jefferson was the second largest slaveholder in Albemarle County, that John Adams ultimately ignored his wife, Abigail's appeal to "remember the ladies" while on his way to the Continental Congress in 1776, or that, collectively, the founders could not conceive of same-gender marriage. The blueprint for the American experiment to sustain itself had been established on July 2, 1776.

The justifiable critique of America's celebration of Independence Day that is in tension with what was espoused in the Declaration of Independence cannot rely on the sophomoric certainty that depends on a sliver of Douglass' words. It is no different than those that conveniently lift a portion of Martin Luther King's keynote address at the 1963 March on Washington because, void of context, it supports their preconceived position. Opposition to a flawed analysis does not, in effect, make it correct. Those utilizing Douglass' words to refute the existing idolatry of the Fourth of July festivities are merely an extension of the same flawed paradigm.

What to the American Slave, or to many of their decedents, is the Fourth of July? To some, given America's complicated history, it suggests these are superfluous extravaganzas that oversimplify a complex narrative. What is the ethos of the Declaration of Independence? It is, and continues to be, the inclusive moral justification to move the nation closer to what it originally committed.

Those opposed to American hypocrisy should continue, as Douglass offered shortly before his death in 1895, when asked what advice he would give to a young black American, "Agitate! Agitate! Agitate!" That can be achieved in the 21st century without the impulse to cheapen Douglass' words for immediate self-satisfaction.

Oh, Martin

Dr. Martin Luther King was, and remains today, in the words of A. Phillip Randolph, "The moral leader of our nation." King's life and work in the public discourse has been analyzed, lionized, idolized, and criticized, but is it understood?

Since King's death, America has applied its standard practice by oversimplifying him in a manner that makes him palatable to a larger swath for public consumption, creating a warring tension between the "Cheap King" and the "Authentic King."

"Oh, Martin" is my letter to the Authentic King who died in 1968, but whose words and philosophy remain relevant in the 21st century.

OH MARTIN, I have so much to tell you. Things have changed since that shot rang out in Memphis on April 4, 1968. You suddenly became more popular in death than you ever were in life. As you know well, before that tragic day in Memphis, you weren't so popular with blacks or whites.

Remember that strange coalition of blacks and whites critical of you when you opposed the war in Vietnam at Riverside Church on April 4, 1967? Surely you recall when the Washington Post and New York Times criticized you on their editorial pages, suggesting that speech had diminished your usefulness to your cause, your country, and your people. Life magazine went as far as calling it "demagogic slander that sounded like a script for Radio Hanoi." There were also myopic Negroes who accused you of linking disparate issues (Vietnam and civil rights). Even young black people felt you were past your prime as they preferred the chants of "Black Power" over your philosophy of nonviolent civil disobedience. It was a veritable rainbow coalition of opposition, many beholden to the dysfunctional guardrails of the status quo, singing in melodic harmony: "Martin, stay in your lane!"

You answered these criticisms and others so eloquently when you stated, "There is something strangely inconsistent about a nation and a press that would praise you when you say, 'Be nonviolent toward (Selma, Alabama Sheriff) Jim Clark,' but will curse and damn you when you say, 'Be nonviolent toward little brown Vietnamese children!'" One year later, all was forgotten. Few of those in opposition took the time to acknowledge that you were indeed ahead of the curve on Vietnam. I believe, however, by the time of your death, you had already witnessed a shift in public opinion.

The aftermath of Vietnam became a data point for America's arrested development—a young nation that fast-tracked its way to superpower status in unprecedented fashion. Martin, you were a truth-teller. Truth-tellers are rarely lauded, especially in their own time. They make society uncomfortable because they often possess a love for society that's so profound, they are unwilling to acquiesce to the preferred conveniences of the status quo. As you stated in your anti-Vietnam address, you spoke out against the war because of your love for the nation. You added, "There can be no great disappointment where there is no deep love." As society focuses on what the nation is, the truth-teller seeks to lift the nation beyond the comforts of its self-induced megalomania, offering a vision of what could be if the nation possessed the necessary courage.

But when you died, the door was left ajar for revisionist history. Actually, it was left open and the door hinges had been removed. The nation mourned—the world mourned—as America, in particular, wrestled with the dilemma of celebrating a truth-teller. That's a paradoxical proposition because in the American narrative, as your life bears witness, truth-tellers are lynched, gunned down, incarcerated, beaten, and marginalized.

Your death couldn't be marginalized. As Langston Hughes' poem, Mother to Son, states: "All the time you and your prophetic truth were a climbin' on, and reachin' landin's, and turnin' corners, and sometimes goin' in dark where there ain't been no light" so that the nation could uncomfortably move closer to its meaning and purpose. Your authentic self couldn't be placed in the prefabricated box of convenience for the nation to gaze in wonderment. For the last half-century, we've embarked on the process of creating a new you—a less threatening, less radical you.

The only way we could get the holiday in your honor was by creating a version of you that was not you—one that would have been palatable to a large swath of the American public. This version offers a plethora of King holiday sales by corporations that portray themselves as being in lockstep with the movement that you gave your life. You are actually a pitchman for multinational corporations that, during your lifetime, would have been unlikely allies to the movement you led. The price for the holiday that began in 1986 wasn't that high, only that we defang, castrate, and domesticate you so that your legacy would rest in the melancholy longings of yesteryear and not something that might result in a movement for radical change today as the logical extension of your work.

The original advocates for the holiday in your honor were not wrong; perhaps naïve to assume America would honor you in your authentic self. Invariably, there are multiple versions for anyone perceived as an American icon. Just as there are multiple versions of Thomas Jefferson, Abraham Lincoln, Thomas Edison, etc., multiple versions exist posthumously of you. While there may be multiple versions, they usually fit in one of two larger categories.

One category, which I will call "Cheap King," borders on perfection, distributed to mass markets, easy to digest, and does not require critical thinking. If anything, it possesses disdain for the latter consideration. This King is deified, the perfect embodiment of the granite statue next to the National Mall in Washington DC—a detached and immovable object that stands above the people he served.

Just as the Lost Cause was largely a historical, fabricated interpretation of the Civil War that attempts to place the Confederacy in the best possible light, Cheap King serves a similar purpose in that it galvanizes the most support while maintaining the aura that only milquetoast transformation is possible. Cheap King doesn't make anyone uncomfortable. Cheap King, as your colleague, Vincent Harding, wrote, is "the gentle, non-abrasive hero whose recorded speeches can be used as inspirational resources for rocking our memories to sleep." Cheap King has the holiday. He is the architect of countless marches to nowhere to commemorate his birth — the spokesperson for myriad corporations from McDonald's to Rolex.

The other version, which I will call the "Authentic King," is complicated — a walking contradiction of high and low moments. Your greatness and foibles were intertwined in a manner that makes you accessible. The version of you that borders on perfection is one we can conveniently fashion in our image. That version of you is used as the puppeteer that sits on our lap as we create the illusion that you're speaking. It is the Authentic King that not only valiantly opposed the Vietnam War when it wasn't popular and wrote the Letter from Birmingham Jail, but used the Declaration of Independence and Constitution to hold the mirror of moral self-reflection for the nation to uncomfortably gaze at. The Authentic King lost his life in Memphis lobbying for the dignity of sanitation workers or, as a Jewish brother I know referred to as the "least of these."

For this latter consideration, it is tragically understandable that a large segment of the nation takes delight in freezing you on August 28, 1963 as the March on Washington's 34-year-old keynote speaker.

Ironically, we still don't know the name of the speech that electrified the crowd and the nation that day. We continue to erroneously call it, "I Have a Dream."

The dominant culture loves to posit: "Dr. King dreamt of a world where one would not be judged by the color of their skin but by the content of their character." Not surprisingly, I have yet to hear any of them suggest as you did on that sweltering August day in the nation's Capitol, "America has given the Negro people a bad check, a check which has come back marked 'insufficient funds'."

Your 17-minute address that critiqued the paradoxical nature of the American experiment as it related to its citizens of color, has been reduced to a final five-minute aspirational stanza designed largely to foster a warm and fuzzy feeling. The greatness of the speech notwithstanding, it has served to fuel our idol worship of the Cheap King without having to engage the Authentic King legacy. The misuse of the "I Have a Dream" mantra has emboldened the Cheap King—a 21st-century shill that justifies rolling back affirmative action who supports the dehumanization of gays and lesbians.

But the March on Washington keynote address was not only your coming out party to the nation, it was tragically the day you became victim of the words, taken from the Letter from Birmingham Jail as you were in effect "harried by day and haunted by night." Because of that speech, you were dubbed by the FBI as "the most dangerous Negro in America," and with the written permission of Attorney General Robert Kennedy, you were surveilled 24 hours per day for the remaining five years of your life.

The government never had a reason to unduly pressure the Cheap King. But the Authentic King was urged by the FBI to commit suicide as a way to thwart sending tapes to your wife, Coretta, when FBI surveillance uncovered your extra-marital affairs. The Authentic King was tired. Though you were only 39 years old when you died, the autopsy placed your age in the mid-60s. I'm not certain FBI Director J. Edgar Hoover would have been so obsessed with the Cheap King. There may not have been assassination attempts on his life.

But America only possesses the bandwidth to honor the Cheap King. There can be no holiday for the Authentic King. It is the Cheap King that most people hold up in social media debates as to whether they side with your philosophy or that of Malcolm X, as if the black freedom struggle did not need both voices. The overly simplistic understanding of your legacy continues to haunt us in the 21st century.

Warring factions play tug-of-war with your legacy. One side offers a misunderstanding of your love ethic to portray you as the jolly little preacher from Atlanta, who provides cover for the evils that the dominant culture participates. The other side offers that in the last year of your life, you finally saw the light and became more militant in the style of Malcolm X. Ultimately, it is a contest over the legacy of the Cheap King.

I fear the Cheap King has become woven into the fabric of America, creating a harmonious relationship of misunderstanding. It seductively uses those presumed to be knowledgeable allies of your movement to call into question methods consistent with the authentic King. In 2016, Atlanta protestors outraged by the police killings of Alton Sterling and Philando Castile used their bodies to shut down a portion of a freeway. Urging for calm, Atlanta Mayor, Kasim Reed, in opposition to the protestor's methods, not far from where you are buried, offered this historical inaccuracy, "Dr. King would never take a freeway." Was he unaware that you led a march from Selma to Montgomery? Did he not know about "Bloody Sunday?" Did the mayor not know direct action was key to any nonviolent campaign? Or was it simply that he was now wearing the hat of the status quo and "law and order" became his primary objective?

Reed, as well as several other notable African Americans, including Oprah Winfrey, aligned their thinking with that of former Republican Arkansas Governor, Mike Huckabee, decrying the protestors as not part of the vaunted status quo. What they failed to reconcile as they lifted up the Cheap King as their defense, the Authentic King, languished in Bull Connor's Jail cell, wrote in his Letter from Birmingham Jail, offering discomfort was a prerequisite for change. Has there ever been a successful movement in America that moved the nation closer to the amorphous "more perfect union" that did so without creating discomfort for the status quo? When invoking the Cheap King, it becomes easy to forget the Authentic King temporarily put the planning for his own Poor People's Campaign on hold to be in Memphis to support the plight of sanitation workers.

When I wrote my book on the events of 1963, I concluded that it has been easier to replicate the hostility of Alabama Governor, George Wallace, than the hope embodied by you. Wallace circa 1963 and his descendants have been largely concerned with the individual pursuit of power under the pretense of faux patriotism. It taps into the unrest of those feeling uneasy by the intangible inevitability of change by providing a tangible enemy to blame. It is not interested in authentically locating the nexus of one's fears. This is reflective of a tragic through line in the nation's history that the quest for change has been invariably challenged by emotional-based arguments that have no intention of making the nation better. In a macro context, is there a connection between Wallace and former President Donald Trump? Though we honor the Cheap King, it is the Authentic Wallace that remains more influential in the public discourse.

I know this is hard to comprehend, but the ethos of George Wallace circa 1963 shows up far more in our contemporary discourse than your "Beloved Community." As you may recall, roughly a week before your assassination, you told Harry Belafonte that you worried whether the aims of the civil rights movement were "integrating into a burning house." But when Belafonte asked what should they do, you replied, "I guess we're just going to have to become firemen." But the valiant to extinguish the blaze have been offset by arsonists seizing every opportunity to gaslight the situation.

America is no longer the burning building that you feared—it has become a reenactment of the Donner Party that believes cannibalism is the only way to survive. Americans routinely view other Americans as existential threats. Marred by a corrosive certainty, too many Americans see the answer to their concerns is to collectively marginalize the individual that sees the world differently. As you well know, historically, empires implode from within.

I'm not sure how you felt about abortion, but the Supreme Court decision in Roe v. Wade, which protected women's rights to an abortion, had not been decided at the time of your death and was recently overturned. Though Roe stood for nearly 50 years, Justice Samuel Alito wrote in his majority opinion, "The inescapable conclusion is that a right to abortion is not deeply rooted in the nation's history and traditions." Future legal scholars may look back on this sentence and conclude this is one of the most egregious legal opinions since Justice Roger Taney invalidated the possibility of citizenship for those of African descent in the Dred Scott decision by stating that African descendants "had no rights which the white man was bound to respect; and that the negro might justly and lawfully be reduced to slavery for his benefit."

Because of the dynamic nature of the American narrative, nothing is deeply rooted until it is. Alito's supposition suggests only the worldview of the framers of the Constitution is deeply held in American history. Only the rights of the original gentry class, which composed roughly 16% of the American population, would be deeply rooted in the "nations history and traditions," as Justice Alito offered.

This rationale appears to be an attack on your life's work. When the Voting Rights Act of 1965 was passed, it was the first time that America could say that every American had equal access to the riches of democracy. In 2013, in the case Shelby County v. Holder, the Supreme Court gutted Section 5 of the VRA, which removed any preclearance requirements from states that necessitated the VRA. In the 21st century Supreme Court decisions have granted corporations certain free speech and freedom of religious protections, implemented further restrictions on gun laws, along with systematic rollbacks on civil liberties.

I dare say that your participation in our public consciousness is to be the moral dummy that sits on our lap while we conveniently put words in your mouth. We forcefully use your words literally, void of any responsibility for context. Even family members, whose legitimacy is bolstered by sharing your last name, use the veneer of your words to promote an ideology adverse to your beliefs. But the Cheap King reigns supreme, popular but useless. He is a standard bearer for the status quo that doesn't possess a transformative ethos. Unlike the Authentic King, the Cheap King is not interested in the redistribution of wealth. I doubt he would break from his busy schedule to aid the plight of sanitation workers in Memphis.

I am sorry to report that your "dream" is but a fleeting memory of yesterday, placed on the life support of annual commemorations as we fawn over the Cheap

King.

Why am I calling it "your dream"? That's how popular culture understands it. What else should we call it?

Maybe that explains why one of the speech's colloquial names is "Martin's Dream." As long as it's your dream, we can laud it without the responsibility to take action—a way to momentarily rent a feel-good impulse.

In your 13-year trek from Montgomery to Memphis, you were praised, criticized, lauded, censured, admired, and harassed. Now, with the assistance of the Cheap King, you are the unwitting victim of idolatry. There were far more supporters of your legacy once you died than the day prior to your assassination. That strange coalition referred earlier assembled at Ebenezer Baptist Church to pay their respects at your funeral. They marched behind your mule-drawn casket, to bury the Authentic King and to begin the resurrection process of the cheap version. So, we now learn about your project through osmosis and sound bites, television advertisements, and quotes taken out of context in order to embrace a morality that does not cause us discomfort, which is the antithesis of change. But without your authenticity to offer the counter-narrative, we can sing praises to the Cheap King; build meaningless monuments to his legacy, void of the burdens for which you gave your life. In the words of the poet, Carl Wendell Hines, Jr., "Dead men make such convenient heroes."

As we collectively cherish your legacy, the warring

factions between the two versions of you create an arrested development. Do we accept the mythology associated with the Cheap King, who is designed to pacify the status quo, defanged and harmless? Or do we embrace the authentic version, whose pursuit of greatness was paved with imperfections?

If the Authentic King was foremost in our thinking, America probably wouldn't have an annual commemoration honoring your birth, but we would be a much better people in a much better place. Alas, both sides of this unfortunate equation are vying for supremacy of your legacy. Your true legacy, therefore, remains hidden under a cacophony of platitudes. I fear the only thing the two camps agree on is the desire to have you do for us posthumously what we really should be doing for ourselves.

Ever mindful that you gave your life in defense of the least of these, I bid you adieu with love, admiration, and appreciation for your profound impact on my project.

Sincerely,

Byron

What is Whiteness?

Defining whiteness in America's color-coded caste system can be akin to calling someone racist. What does one mean when they say it? What does one hear when it's said? Is it a one-size-fits-all classification? Or like other matters in America's public discourse, does any attempt to define whiteness require nuance and circumspection?

WHAT IS WHITENESS? Is it a race, an amorphous social construct, or a Faustian bargain? However defined, the notion of whiteness sits at the pinnacle of a pernicious caste system, infecting the soul of every American. The insidious application of whiteness is the nation's paramount consideration, ahead of its stated civic virtues of liberty and equality, per the Declaration of Independence. As James Baldwin suggests in "*On Being 'White' and Other Lies,*" there is no white community per se. There is no central headquarters where one can protest its myriad grievances. Whiteness exists as a decentralized fortress of solidarity, where one may enter only by invitation. It is best defined, not by who is white, but rather by who is not. Moreover, whiteness as I am defining it, is ultimately a male-centric enterprise.

Throughout American history, whiteness has operated on dual tracks—protectionist and reactionary. The former consideration is grounded in the primary objective of whiteness, which is maintaining a status quo. I do not posit all white people knowingly participate in the concept of whiteness. But as with all forms of established American privilege, whiteness is normalized in the culture so that its benefits can often go without notice.

The reactionary track, though subordinate to the protectionist objectives, is perhaps the more obvious and is often conducted by those who are not the ultimate beneficiaries of whiteness. Caught in the vice grip between America's commitments and those who seek to redeem their long overdue promissory note, the reactionary coalition operates as if the expansion of equality is a finite resource that must come at their expense. Their allegiance to whiteness over the centuries has led many to disregard policies where they might realize personal gain for fear that nonwhites might also benefit.

The Faustian Bargain

Whiteness predates the formalization of America as a sovereign nation. Therefore, the immortal words, "We hold these truths to be self-evident that all men are created equal," were truncated to fit within the paradigm of whiteness. Committing to the word "all" as in "all men are created equal" was a paradoxical proposition that proved difficult to coexist with the institution of whiteness. It becomes the vehicle by which those who call themselves white would learn to accept the otherwise unacceptable.

When America held its first election in 1788,

according to the National Archives, only 6% of the population possessed the voting franchise. [The estimated percentage of those disenfranchised at the nation's inception commonly ranges between 94%-84%.] Though not expressly stated in the Constitution, most states held that only landowning white males could vote. How might a nation commit to a radical mission statement of liberty and equality while sanctioning inequality to roughly 94% of the populace?

On March 31, 1776, roughly 90 days before America formally declared its secession from Great Britain, Abigail Adams wrote to her husband and one of the artisans of the Declaration, John, stating, "I long to hear that you have declared an independency -- and by the way in the new Code of Laws which I suppose it will be necessary for you to make I desire you would Remember the Ladies, and be more generous and favourable to them than your ancestors. Do not put such unlimited power into the hands of the Husbands. Remember all Men would be tyrants if they could."

This appeal—one of the earliest in the American narrative to formally lobby for women's suffrage—fell on deaf ears. Debates on this omission traditionally hover around the founders were merely "men of their times" and the main goal was independence from Britain, therefore, they could ill-afford to get bogged down in what was perceived as ancillary issues. These arguments are plausible, but the omission, as well as others, further crystallized in practice, placing white male landowners atop America's democratic food chain.

State laws in the 18th and early 19th centuries

bestowed voting rights exclusively to white male landowners. It was an all-or-nothing proposition. Achieving two-thirds of the criteria, though insufficient to attain full citizenship, was perceived as superior in comparison to all who were not white males. This was the genesis of a *Faustian* bargain whereby being white would be codified. Property laws were critical to the newly formalized United States—a carryover from the British legal tradition. By extending the definition of property to include married men, the notion of white male landowners simultaneously became more inclusive for many white males, but more prohibiting to everyone else. This gesture of inclusivity bestowed to white males, who might otherwise be disenfranchised, provided adjunct status into the fraternity of whiteness, creating an allegiance based more on skin color than the nation's civic virtue.

To support this incongruence, it would require that America justify its position sociologically, scientifically, and legally, declaring those in bondage were subhuman and, therefore, did not qualify as recipients of liberty or equality. The sociology necessitated the obvious difference based on skin color. It is here that gave rise to "whiteness" becoming a social construct, synonymous with superiority. No matter how far adrift low-income whites were from America's civic commitments, they could always take slender satisfaction in knowing they were white. This notion necessitated that African Americans be rendered to a permanent place of inferiority, allowing all whites, regardless of their social station, to be pacified by the knowledge that there was an entrenched group that dwelled beneath.

In the 18th century, European philosophers and scientists were putting forth the notion that mental differences existed between races. Scientific racism was a key component to legitimize white supremacy. Nineteenth-century scientists, like Harvard's Louis Agassiz, championed "polygenism," which held that human races were distinct species. This theory was supported by pseudoscientific methods like craniometry, the measurement of human skulls, which attempted to demonstrate whites were biologically superior to blacks. Scientific racism was a misappropriated exercise to bolster the case for whiteness with pseudo-intellectual heft.

The final leg of this macabre triumvirate was the Supreme Court's *Dred Scott* decision (1857). Chief Justice Roger Taney, writing for the majority, opined that a black man had no rights that a white man was bound to respect. According to Taney, black people could not be citizens anywhere within America's jurisdiction. The Dred Scott legalized sociological and scientific pursuits.

Furthering this Faustian agreement is the levy exacted upon those deemed as white. One may acknowledge one's cultural origins, be it German, Irish, French, etc., within their local communities, but in their larger world, they must assume the non-descript persona of whiteness if they are to receive all rights and privileges thereunto and pertaining. As the United States methodically prepared to enter WWI in 1917, former President Theodore Roosevelt speaking to the largely Irish Catholic Knights of Columbus at Carnegie

Hall on Columbus Day 1915, asserted:

"There is no room in this country for hyphenated Americanism. When I refer to hyphenated Americans, I do not refer to naturalized Americans. Some of the very best Americans I have ever known were naturalized Americans, Americans born abroad. But a hyphenated American is not an American at all ... The one absolutely certain way of bringing this nation to ruin, of preventing all possibility of its continuing to be a nation at all, would be to permit it to become a tangle of squabbling nationalities, an intricate knot of German-Americans, Irish-Americans, English-Americans, French-Americans, Scandinavian-Americans or Italian-Americans, each preserving its separate nationality, each at heart feeling more sympathy with Europeans of that nationality, than with the other citizens of the American Republic ... There is no such thing as a hyphenated American who is a good American. The only man who is a good American is the man who is an American and nothing else."

Roosevelt made clear the standard admission for whiteness in the nation's geopolitical pursuits. Moreover, failure to acquiesce resulted in violence, particularly against German-Americans, who sustained ghoulish treatment during WWI that became the precursor for the treatment of Japanese Americans, particularly on the West Coast during WWII. Whiteness, therefore, as writer James Baldwin opines, "is a moral choice. For there are no white people."

On the Backs of Blacks

As newly arriving 19th-century European immigrants to America were greeted with social hostility, there was always a possible off-ramp that was not available to those whose phenotype bore a darker hue. In Toni Morrison's "On the Backs of Blacks," she opens by describing a scene from Elia Kazan's *America, America*. In the film's final scene, Morrison juxtaposes Stavros' shining shoes in Grand Central Station with a young black man who is doing similar. Stavros, seemingly learning the ways of America, literally blocks the door, simultaneously stern and congenial until he receives a tip from the appreciative patron. In the previous scene, the young black man is also shining a patron's shoes, but he is promptly run off. The juxtaposition could not be starker as the young black man is treated like society's scourge, while Stavros is buoyed by possibilities that await, especially if he is willing to exchange his rich Greek heritage for the nondescript vanilla flavoring of whiteness.

"How the Irish Became White", written by Noel Ignatiev, describes the odyssey how many fled Ireland and British oppression beginning in the 18th century, arriving to America at the bottom of the European hierarchy, facing nativist discrimination, and eventually gaining social acceptance. Ironically, the narrative offers newly arriving Irish and free African Americans lived in proximity. For the Irish, as with other newly arriving European immigrants, being despised was a temporary assignment that would expire over time. "The most harmful consequence," Ignatiev writes, "of the slave system was the production of free Negroes. Free Negroes were a dangerous class because it would be impossible for blacks in the North ever to be reconciled with whites while hundreds of thousands of their countryman are bleeding and dying in the South." On the basis of whiteness, the origins of America's greatest challenge (the Civil War) were not the attempts to coexist with the paradox of creating a nation based on the ideals of liberty and equality while sanctioning inequality, but to blame those victimized by the incongruence based on skin color.

Though daunting and, at times, abusive, the Irish extricated themselves from the dungeon of America's social hierarchy. But for people of color, blacks in particular, scorned for being "other" was a permanent position. Part of the Irish's formal admission into whiteness included overt hostility to African Americans.

In 1964, former attorney general, Robert Kennedy, who coincidentally came from an Irish family that many Americans would regard as royalty in an American context, stated that in 40 years, a black man could be President of the United States.

On February 18, 1965, writer, James Baldwin, during a debate with William F. Buckley at the University of Cambridge, offered the following assessment of Kennedy's remarks:

"I remember when the ex-Attorney General, Mr. Robert Kennedy said that it was conceivable that in 40 years in America, we might have a Negro president. And that sounded like a very emancipated statement, I suppose, to white people. They were not in Harlem when this statement was first heard. They did not hear, and possibly will never hear the bitterness and scorn with which this statement was greeted. From the point of view of the man in the Harlem barbershop, Bobby Kennedy only got here yesterday. And now he's already on his way to the presidency. We've (African Americans) been here for 400 years and now he tells us that maybe in 40 years, if we're good we may let you become president."

The Seductive Influence of Whiteness

Comedian, Chris Rock, during one of his sold-out standup performances, stated: "There ain't a white man in this room that would trade places with me. None of you would change places with me, and I'm rich! That's how good it is to be white." Rock's searing comedic critique places a historical spotlight on the incongruence between the influence of whiteness and its ultimate beneficiaries.

Whiteness needs the black face as a soothing balm of acceptance that pacifies white people who have yet to take advantage of the presumed largesse of whiteness. This is the point of Douglass Turner Ward's 1965 play,

OUR AMERICAN EXPERIMENT

Day of Absence—the farcical story of a southern town where all of its black residents vanish. The town is hurled into chaos, not only because of the impact of racial capitalism and the reliance on cheap exploitable labor represented by the black body, but also, without the black face, whom would those in the bottom quartile of whiteness have to look down upon? Whiteness relies on the black face to maintain social order. In Douglass' narrative, whiteness depends upon a morbid objectification where the black body is desperately needed to successfully fulfill the gaps created by America's ongoing economic need for cheap exploitable labor, while symbolically representing of the unforgiving basement in America's social hierarchy. Is that not the purpose of 21st-century hot-button issues such as opposition to the 1619 Project, critical race theory, and "wokeism"? It matters little that disagreements are not clearly articulated. The aforementioned issues are identified with having a black face. Moreover, as Professor Carol Anderson offers in *Burning Down Brown*, over the centuries, low-income whites are willing to seemingly vote against their economic self-interests. The implied assumption is economic concerns are primary to these voters. Their economic self-interest, in my view, holds a secondary position to maintain their understanding of the status quo. This is one of the central themes of Thomas Frank's 2004 bestseller, "*What's the Matter with Kansas*?" Or as former President Lyndon Johnson observed: "If you can convince the lowest white man he's better than the best colored man, he won't notice you're picking his pocket.

Hell, give him somebody to look down on and he'll empty his pockets for you."

Historically, this has meant supporting second-class citizenship for nonwhites, accepting debunked concepts under the guise of constitutional legitimacy (Interposition and Nullification), and on many occasions, supporting local laws adrift from any understanding of the Constitution. But destructive laws designed to maintain "social structure" have infiltrated into unsuspecting communities that offered unwavering support, also bringing unintended consequences. As Anderson notes, it was the southern states that fought the 1954 landmark Supreme Court ruling Brown v. Board of Education the hardest and found themselves at the bottom quartile of state rankings for educational attainment, per capita income, and quality of health. This too has taken on different facets throughout the centuries, but is nevertheless a consistent thread in the American narrative. It appears to be a small sacrifice to maintain the status quo of whiteness.

White Rage

White rage is often viewed as synonymous with whiteness. A derivative of whiteness, white rage is the response to maintain the status quo no matter how far afield the present moment one may be from the nation's civic virtue. In spite of its inflammatory moniker, white rage does not necessarily equate to violence. It can appear in forms of violence as well as nonviolence. Lynchings, church bombings, police dogs, fire hoses, and the Ku Klux Klan are violent tools of white rage, but voter suppression in its myriad forms and bank redlining are examples of its genteel sibling. Paradoxically, white rage has been the response throughout the American narrative when a group deemed outside the white male paradigm seeks to move the nation closer to its stated values. White rage is the mechanism that reasserts whiteness at the zenith of America's social organization chart. Historically, this is a useless exercise because the expansion of America's promise of equality has never come at the expense of others. It is effective, however, in its ability to make race the preeminent barometer, rather than other social and economic variables.

Naiveté

Anderson notes the sense of elation that NAACP Director, Roy Wilkins, experienced immediately following the *Brown* decision dissipated once he realized the extent that the status quo—particularly but not exclusively in the South—was willing to maintain their understanding of normalcy. The South viewed the Brown decision with nearly the same unsettling feelings that prompted 11 southern states to secede from the Union shortly after Abraham Lincoln was elected president in 1860. "My sense of euphoria was a bit naïve," Wilkins lamented.

But Wilkins' naiveté is as old as the republic because he, like many men and women who came before him, assumed once those seeking meaningful change overcame a particular hurdle, the riches of justice would finally be available. Wilkins, immediately after the Brown decision, couldn't see the Southern Manifesto on the horizon any more than many could see the Ku Klux Klan would become an accepted "Christian" organization in the early 20th century in 1865. Given America's documented history of white rage, how many saw the emergence of Donald J. Trump as the nation's 46th president on January 20, 2009 when Barack Obama took the oath of office for the first time?

Underestimation is an indispensable ally to white rage. *Brown* provided the predicate for the nation moving forward. Those who did not like the Supreme Court's ruling found methods to disregard the gist of the decision. Wilkins' naiveté is linked to Martin Luther King's appeal on April 3, 1968, "All we say to America is be true to what you said on paper." Historically, the opponents to change, as Wilkins' dismay bears witness, have only adhered to King's simplistic demand, after trying everything else to the contrary to maintain a dysfunctional status quo.

Varying from intimidation to pernicious laws to ignoring the nation's committed values, the goal remains the same—stagnate progress to maintain the status quo. How many black soldiers who fought in the Civil War, the Spanish American War, along with World Wars I and II, believed their valor on the battlefield abroad would unlock the doors to full citizenship at home? How many held that belief as they were being lynched by welcoming white mobs while still in uniform?

How does one explain Red Summer in 1919? Coined by writer, James Weldon Johnson, Red Summer was a series of racial conflicts across the United States where whites indiscriminately attacked Negroes. It resulted in hundreds of deaths, countless injuries, and the annihilation of Negro property and businesses. Tensions resulting from the postwar expectations held by many Negroes fueled white social fears, labor unrest as industrialists used Negroes as strikebreaking pawns to threaten white workers who were fighting for better working conditions, further stoking racial resentment. Communist fears, unsubstantiated claims of linking Negroes to anarchist efforts, the government's overt messages of who was truly American, and its tacit approval through its silence legitimized the violence.

Beyond the social construct of whiteness, the institution of slavery, and Jim Crow laws rest the desperation to believe a fallacious yarn rooted in biological superiority. It has necessitated the creation of a coalition that eschews every consideration except one: whiteness. By granting this distinction a place of vaunted superiority, the perceived progress of groups outside this domain becomes assumed as an existential threat to its survival. This, in my view, explains in a contemporary context why low-income whites seemingly vote against their economic self-interests. Their economic self-interest holds a secondary position to maintain their understanding of the status quo.

Conclusion

BYRON WILLIAMS

The African American experience for myriad reasons is often the historical data point used in any discussion of whiteness. Well-heeled white males, notwithstanding, no group in America possesses a legacy immune from the toxic grip of whiteness. Though on the surface it appears paradoxical and incongruent, whiteness has been woven into the American fabric so that the montage that is the American experiment endowed by liberty and equality is presented as a quilt that bears only a single fabric.

Whiteness has enjoyed a long run in the American narrative. I suspect it will continue until there is an internal commitment to change or it simply experiences diminishing returns. The latter distinction seems less likely because the true recipients of whiteness have always been fewer than those who participate to protect its virtue. As recent history indicates, it may splinter into additional reactionary factions, which will most likely be more virulent in their hatred, but ultimately will continue to serve the interest of its protectionist brethren. Beyond a social construct or Faustian bargain, the orthodoxy of whiteness is far more intrinsic and insidious within the American narrative. Whiteness, as Baldwin offers, remains "a moral choice."

AFTERWORD

There is a famous line from John Ford's Western drama, *The Man Who Shot Liberty Valance*:

"When the legend becomes fact, print the legend."

This quote accurately captures the essence of the American narrative, in my view.

Not only has America printed the preferred legend, but it has also become a basis by which contemporary issues are debated and understood. This is to be expected. Like Ford's epic Western that delves into the nuanced complexities of good, evil, and morality, along with the tension created when the concocted story stands adjacent to reality, America has a complicated story embodying similar attributes.

America is arguably the most radical undertaking of any democratic form of government because it rests on an idea—the idea of coalescing liberty and equality into a singular unifying force. Over the centuries, this unprecedented creed has been ensnarled by the instincts of insularity, avarice, greed, self-righteousness, and fear.

I penned these texts because I believe, in 2023, as did Franklin Roosevelt in 1936, this generation of Americans has a rendezvous with destiny. The alternative may be to forgo any pretense to the commitments made on July 4, 1776.

Though the subjects presented in this essay collection vary, they do point to one merging theme— the American project is not a canonized idea, but a complex mosaic. The American narrative is not the sole possession of any group or orthodoxy. In fact, "the" American narrative rests just beyond anyone's full comprehension.

Fearing what we don't understand represents cowardly participation in the American project. It is relying on the empty calories of privilege to ignore the reasons why someone can see the same event differently. When looting occurred in some of the protests associated with the Black Lives Matter efforts, while one cannot be an apologist for breaking the law, one is also burdened with understanding what gave rise to the demonstrations. Judicious understanding cannot occur by simply holding tightly to our preferred narrative. Critical issues usually do not present themselves so neatly.

The challenge when merely printing the legend is that it demands nothing from us beyond acceptance or rejection. It creates linear suppositions that demand nuance and circumspection. With the futility akin to boxing water, we often debate contemporary issues supported by the sinking sand of the flawed narrative.

In this critical juncture of American history, we

must also grapple with the paradoxical question: Are the issues we're debating really the issues? Are they merely tools of obfuscation camouflaging what rests at the epicenter of concern? If, as James Baldwin opined, "American history is longer, larger, more various, more beautiful, and more terrible than anything anyone has ever said about it," it is incumbent upon each of us to reach down into the paradoxical morass to struggle with all aspects of Baldwin's analysis. It is only there that one can realize the greatness of the American project.

~ BW